Doreen Fleet

Creative Interventions in Counselling and Psychotherapy

A Pluralistic and Humanist Approach

palgrave
macmillan

Doreen Fleet
University of Chester
Chester, UK

ISSN 2662-9127 ISSN 2662-9135 (electronic)
Palgrave Texts in Counselling and Psychotherapy
ISBN 978-3-032-16608-1 ISBN 978-3-032-16609-8 (eBook)
https://doi.org/10.1007/978-3-032-16609-8

Cover credit: Elena Vagengeym/alamy

This Palgrave Macmillan imprint is published by the registered company Springer Nature Switzerland AG
The registered company address is: Gewerbestrasse 11, 6330 Cham, Switzerland

Palgrave Texts in Counselling and Psychotherapy

Series Editors

David Pocock, Psychoanalytic Psychotherapist &
Systematic Family Therapist, Calne, Wiltshire, UK
Jeremy Woodcock, Holman's Cottage, Nailsworth, UK

This series introduces readers to the theory and practice of counselling and psychotherapy across a wide range of topical issues. Ideal for both trainees and practitioners, the books will appeal to anyone wishing to use counselling and psychotherapeutic skills and will be particularly relevant to workers in health, education, social work and related settings. The books in this series emphasise an integrative orientation weaving together a variety of models including, psychodynamic, attachment, trauma, narrative and systemic ideas. The books are written in an accessible and readable style with a focus on practice. Each text offers theoretical background and guidance for practice, with creative use of clinical examples.

Statement on the Use of Case Studies:

The author has received prior consent to include each case study in the text. Additionally, some minor details have been altered and pseudonyms have been used to protect anonymity.

Contents

About the Author

Dr. Doreen Fleet is a Chartered Psychologist and a BACP (Accred.) Psychotherapist. She began private practice as a counsellor in 2006 and was a Senior Lecturer for Staffordshire University between 2008 and 2020, and was a Senior Fellow with the Higher Education Academy. Currently, she is an External Ph.D. Research Supervisor with Chester University and offers research supervision to both doctoral and MSc students. In her therapeutic practice, she offers both individual and group work. She has consistently used creative ways of working throughout her counselling and teaching career.

Her book on Pluralistic Sand-tray Therapy was published by Routledge, and she has several research papers published in a range of academic journals. With regard to social media activity, in July 2023, Doreen had an article published in Psyche magazine entitled, "Sand-tray therapy can reach the edge of awareness", edited by Christian Jarrett. In the same year, Doreen was interviewed by Damian Mark Smith from Therapist to Millions in a Podcast entitled, 'Exploring Sandbox Therapy'. Then, in October, Doreen delivered a Webinar for the Safer Society Foundation in the USA entitled, "How sand-tray therapy can aid treatment with clients. Doreen is also an avid user of LinkedIn, promoting her work and research, and connecting with other professionals interested in creative work in therapy…".

List of Images

1

Introduction

Creativity opens up new horizons...There is connection to what I've been, what I am and what I intend to be

(Fisher & Specht, 1999, p. 469)

When a person engages in creative discovery in therapy, they might begin with a vague idea of what to explore. Furthermore, there might be no pre-planned goal or specific aim in mind. For example, a client may say, 'I don't know why I have such a low opinion of myself; my parents always say it's just the way I am.' Creative exploration involving a client's intra-psychic experience can result in developing fresh insight into the root cause of their psychological distress; recovery can then become a possibility as they may begin to adopt a different perspective.

At other times, a client may have a nonverbal sense of something, yet unable to find 'their' right words to describe that experience. Gendlin called this the implicit, "a vague, fuzzy, not recognized as a distinct emotion or a familiar feeling" and although they cannot find their words to describe that experience, "it is sensed distinctly" (Gendlin, 1996, p. 18). Creative work that produces symbols representing this implicit sense can aid 'edge of awareness' discovery, that experience existing in the

D. Fleet, *Creative Interventions in Counselling and Psychotherapy*, Palgrave Texts in Counselling and Psychotherapy, https://doi.org/10.1007/978-3-032-16609-8_1

"border zone between the conscious and unconscious" (Gendlin, 1996, pp. 17–18), helping the client to gain insight and alleviate psychological distress.

Moreover, I have worked with clients who have insight into the root cause of their distress, such as having a problematic childhood and yet still suffering anxiety as an adult. However, with the therapist's help in working creatively, the client's inner exploration can facilitate the expression of unresolved hurt, increasing the possibility of a move towards closure. The client can then begin to adopt a new perspective on life, sometimes giving them hope and a sense of relief. Thus, such creative discovery can take a client to the past, present, or a hoped-for future. In line with Fisher and Specht (1999), such insight can bring a connection to what a person has been, what they are currently, and what they hope to be in the future. This process can help them break free from a currently restricted self-concept or dissociated emotions that may have held them back for some time.

There are various definitions of Creativity. May (1994) defines Creativity as a constructive process of "bringing something new into being" (p. 37).

Furthermore, Runco (2014) argued that "Creativity may be encouraged (and blocks to Creativity removed) through actual therapy" (p. 37). Therefore, a client who learns to engage in the creative process during therapy will likely experience a new way of self-expression. Runco (2014) suggested that "one of the best things a person can do to maintain health is to find opportunities for self-expression" (p. 121), and Bandura (1997) stated, "Creativity constitutes one of the highest forms of human expression" (p. 239). Therefore, a client who engages in creative methods in therapy and edge-of-awareness discovery (Gendlin, 1996), thereby bringing fresh insight, may express their issues more effectively.

Similarly, Runco (2014) stated, "One of the most powerful broadly applicable tactics for creative thinking involves a shift of perspective…this shift makes it easy to find original ideas and solutions" (p. 340). Dollinger et al. (2004), in line with this thinking, suggested how openness to experience is linked to Creativity.

Creative therapy can result in a phenomenological shift (Fleet, 2019, 2023, p. 38; Fleet et al., 2021) for the client, as insight and understanding bring a new perspective, involving change in thoughts and emotion, leading to a subsequent sense of hope and self-acceptance. Such hope and self-acceptance often result in a reduction in the client's emotional and psychological distress. Likewise, Runco (2014) discussed how insight involves a shift that provides "a-ha feeling" (p. 29), "and perhaps satisfaction, relief or even surprise" (Gruber Davis, 1988).

Creative methods are conducive to the pluralistic approach, as the therapist is not constrained to working in a way stipulated by the underpinning theoretical approach, unlike some other orientations. The pluralistic approach is based on humanistic assumptions; it is committed to "conceptualizing and engaging with people in a deeply valuing and respectful way" (Cooper, 2007, p. 11) and collaborating with the client, tailoring the therapy "to the particular wants and understandings and engage with the client as a unique and unsystematizable being" (Cooper & McLeod, 2011, p. 17). The approach views value in drawing on ideas and methods from other approaches. For example, creative methods may involve:

- Using colour in a breathing strategy.
- An image to represent a block for a client who feels unable to express emotion.
- Using personal photographs to explore a negative self-image.

Creative discovery can help clients become more authentic and in accord with their organismic experience (Greenberg, 2004). Maslow (1971) and Rogers (1961, 1995) associated creativity with self-actualisation and tied this to psychological health. Natalie Rogers et al. (2012), who advocated for creativity in therapy, suggested that art materials also serve as a medium. These authors likened the use of art materials in therapy to a language of self-expression, just as words are (2012).

However, some therapists in the field of counselling and psychotherapy have a reluctance to use creative methods in their practice with adult clients. Moreover, therapists who offer creative methods to clients can be challenged by those with a self-concept tied to an adult persona and their internalised rules about self-expression. This inhibition can negatively impact "their spontaneity in therapy" (Malchiodi, 2005, p. 13), often refusing any invitation to work creatively.

Therapist reluctance can be based on the humanistic argument that therapy should be about 'being rather than doing'. Greenberg (2004) challenged this stance, arguing that the being-doing dichotomy is inaccurate.

I support Greenberg's stance and suggest that a counsellor can be with the client as they engage in creative exploration, demonstrated by their responses to the client's verbal and creative expressions, and gestures.

Runco (2014) explored the bias concerning the intellectual expectations of adults in Western society and suggested that this begins in the classroom, with teachers predominantly favouring more cognitive learning strategies when teaching children. Torrance et al. (1989) advocated for creative exploration with adults, arguing that it had health-promoting benefits. These authors advised older adults to question and free themselves from society's expectations of how to behave. Unfortunately, once this bias towards cognitive-focused learning is reinforced in childhood, adults who have internalised such expectations tend to avoid playful, creative processing and routinely adopt a serious approach to solving any problem. Therefore, when an adult comes to therapy and is offered creative methods, the therapist may face strong resistance, and no amount of convincing may prompt the adult to be open to new, creative ways of working through their issues. However, the pluralistic therapist will collaborate with clients and respect a client's autonomy when they decide not to try a method that does not align with who they are. Therefore, any creative approach to working is presented as an offer for consideration, and respect is given to a client who states that they do not wish to work in that way. Respecting the client's unique way of being and personal autonomy is at the core of the approach, which aligns with the humanistic stance that views the client's input as essential to the therapeutic process (Cooper & McLeod, 2007).

Cooper and McLeod (2007) suggest how the pluralistic approach values "otherness" (p. 7). Clients are viewed as "active, meaning-oriented beings with a right to self-determination" (p. 7). Taking this humanistic assumption into account, a collaborative approach is essential. The question of "What do clients want?" (p. 7) is central when establishing goals, tasks and methods for therapy. Therefore, it is crucial that the therapist engages the client in dialogue at each stage of the therapy, from assessment to the end of therapy feedback sessions (Cooper & McLeod, 2007), to honour the client's self-determination adhering to the humanistic principle of self-autonomy. During the initial session with a client, a two-way discussion will occur regarding the client's goals and expectations for therapy. The therapist will ask purposeful questions to help the client communicate what they hope to gain from therapy.

Cooper and McLeod (2007) suggest how the pluralistic approach values "otherness" (p. 7). Clients are viewed as "active, meaning-oriented beings" and collaboration between therapist and client is essential.

The question of "What do clients want?" (p. 7) is central when establishing goals, tasks and methods for therapy. Therefore, it is crucial that the therapist engages the client in dialogue at each stage of the therapy, from assessment to the end of therapy feedback sessions (Cooper & McLeod, 2007), to honour the client's self-determination. During the initial session with a client, the therapist will ask purposeful questions to help the client communicate what they hope to gain from therapy.

Goals may be specific, such as wanting to improve their self-confidence in relationships. A task for a client might be to set the goal of saying 'No' more often to others who make demands on them and discuss whether they would be willing to try a creative method to develop this ability.

For example, the creative task may involve the client working on an exercise focusing on 'give and take' in relationships in their own time prior to the next therapy session. In this activity, the client will explore their personal boundaries in current relationships. In the following therapy session, it will be clear whether the task has been completed, and the therapist will discuss with the client how they experienced that exercise, exploring any insights gained. At other times during a session, the same issue may be explored by the client sharing historical examples that contribute to their lack of self-confidence, which might act as a block to them getting their needs met in the present. By the therapist offering empathy, compassion, and understanding, the client can begin to develop their self-confidence.

In my own experience with clients who engage with creative methods, they begin to explore their phenomenological experience. Often, this can create an environment where they can work at their 'edge of awareness' (Gendlin, 1996), and such exploration can also involve the client's configurations of Self (Cooper et al., 2004; Mearns & Thorne, 2000). Those parts within the psyche that are primarily healthy and only become a problem when they dissociate (Cooper et al., 2004). An example is the 'Inner Child', and many of my clients have benefited from creative exploration of this aspect of Self. Whitfield (1987) described how this real aspect of the Self (Inner Child) becomes buried in the unconscious in order to survive due to traumatic childhood experiences. For the adult to recover, unconscious experiences need to be processed through conscious exploration and the expression of repressed emotions.

Such exploration of a client's intra-psychic experience, sometimes using symbols to represent their inner world, can bring insight, foster understanding, and lead to a reduction in psychological and emotional distress.

Hawker (2006) described the function of symbols as "representing ideas or qualities" (p. 710). The use of symbols and metaphors is not a new concept in psychotherapy. Freud (1856–1939), the father of psychoanalysis, used the symbol of the iceberg to communicate the vastness of the unconscious (incorporating the preconscious just beneath the waterline) relating to the immense section below the water, compared to the conscious mind, symbolised by the tip of the iceberg above the water (Freud, 1924, p. 306). The vast unconscious, having a significant influence on a person's behaviour and attitudes, and bringing aspects of it into conscious awareness for processing in therapy, is an excellent opportunity for change.

Clients often use creative symbols in therapy to communicate the intensity of their experiences when representing their inner world, including "personal history, personal relationships, and wider social and cultural experience, aiding interpersonal and intra-psychic processing" (Fleet, 2023, p. 21). For example, a client may refer to a butterfly as a symbol of change, representing their growth and reduced emotional and psychological distress by the end of therapy.

Jungian Sandplay therapists suggest that a creative way of working, using physical objects that symbolise a client's experience, is placed in the sand tray. Jungian therapists suggest how this creative process can access the deepest levels of the unconscious mind, and the conflict existing within the psyche can then be explored (Kalff, 1980; Turner, 2005).

The founder of the Jungian approach, Carl Jung (1972), adopted another form of creative work, using mandalas in therapy. He described this as a creative way of attempting healing "that doesn't spring from conscious reflection but by instinctive impulse" (Jung, 1959, p. 4), suggesting the significance of the unconscious mind.

My view aligns with the Jungian approach regarding the use of creative symbols and how they can offer a powerful representation of the client's experience that words alone cannot convey. Working creatively can help a client explore the meaning of that symbol in-depth, processing emotional expression and self-understanding of an issue that was not previously entirely in conscious awareness. For example, a client who enjoys drawing might be motivated to illustrate that symbol, and then free writing can help them engage in deeper reflection. The therapist can then assist the client in reflecting further on their creative work, helping them connect to their past, present, and future life experiences.

In my case study research, which involved delivering Pluralistic Sand-Tray Therapy (Fleet, 2023), in the final session, Ruth placed a butterfly object into the sand to represent her progress, specifically a decrease in her emotional and psychological distress. Ruth was very animated as she described how she felt much happier and had a more positive outlook on her life, "It helped me to talk about things from my past, put that to bed now" (Fleet, 2019, 2023, p. 20), indicating how she gained a sense of closure concerning her difficult childhood. In Ruth's case she experienced a phenomenological shift (Fleet, 2019, 2023; Fleet et al., 2021) as there was a shift in her thoughts, attitudes and emotions bringing a sense of healing and relief.

Although it is more helpful to stay close to the client's interpretation of a symbol, as the therapist's interpretation can differ from the client's, some symbols have a shared meaning that different clients often use to represent their experiences. For example, the butterfly emerging from the cocoon is a powerful symbol of change, and Hefferon et al. (2010) used this to represent a client's post-traumatic growth.

Some scholars (Killick et al., 2016; Stoddard & Afari, 2014) argue that the spoken word, using metaphor, is also a practical, creative way of working in therapy and "is a central tool of the therapist of many therapeutic modalities" (Killick et al., 2016, p. 1 1). Killick refers to metaphors used to describe anger, such as a person being 'fuming' or needing to 'let off steam', which adds richness to the spoken word, giving a more vivid picture of the pressure building up and the intensity of the associated emotion (Killick et al., 2016, p. 2).

Stoddard and Afari, from an Acceptance and Commitment therapeutic stance (ACT) (2014), state how "metaphors make abstract concepts concrete by providing a rich verbal context that evokes thoughts, feelings and behaviours similar to those evoked by the client's actual situation" (p. 16). Furthermore, they argue that experiential metaphors focus on aspects of a person's experience that may go unnoticed in their "real world environment" (p. 17). This approach focuses on the therapist delivering the metaphor to the client in an experiential way, and Stoddard and Afari provide several examples in their work (2014). The metaphor of attempting to 'drive in a thick fog, it being difficult to see where they are going' can be offered to a client who is depressed and unmotivated (Stoddard & Afari, 2014, pp. 22–27).

Working creatively is a common feature of other therapeutic approaches. For example, Natalie Rogers, the daughter of the late Carl Rogers (1902–1987), advocated creative practice from a Person-Centred perspective (PCT) (Rogers, 2000). She expanded her father's work on the six necessary and sufficient conditions for therapeutic personality change (Rogers, 1957, p. 96). She added the condition of the therapist "offering stimulating and challenging experiences" (Rogers, 2000, p. 17) to facilitate creative discovery. Natalie Rogers argued that creativity serves as a medium for self-expression, just as words do. Silverstone (1997), another advocate for creative practice when adopting the person-centred approach, suggested how words alone can present a limitation in therapy.

However, a person-centred therapist will avoid making any interpretations of the client's creative output. Polanyi (1958) argued that the therapist needs to indwell into the client's phenomenological world.

Other stances, such as the psychodynamic approach, suggest how some clients are so well defended that a direct intervention involving therapist interpretations would be necessary to challenge any defence.

Working creatively from a psychodynamic perspective dates back to Freud's dream analysis (1900). Freud perceived dreams to be a highly significant feature when delivering psychoanalysis to his patients. He suggested that when a person dreams, their ego defences are lowered and unconscious material comes through to awareness, although distorted (Freud, 1900). Freud's approach of free association in dreams was a strategy for gaining insight into internal unconscious conflicts, aiming to promote psychological well-being.

Every human being dreams each night (Coolidge et al., 2006). Following Freud's work on dreams, this phenomenon has been a focus of numerous psychological and therapeutic approaches, including those of Jung (1974),Perls (1969), and Taylor (1992). Each theoretical stance adopted a different view of how to work with a client's dream. As a pluralistic therapist, I have often worked with the symbolic nature of a client's dreams, adapting various methods and collaborating with the client.

Creative practice is also a feature of cognitive behavioural therapy (CBT). For example, Thomas (2016) utilises mental imagery to help restructure a client's self-perceptions, viewing this as a link between rational and imaginative thinking. Thomas uses the metaphor of a path and facilitates the client in a visualisation by asking questions to help them express their thoughts and feelings related to the difficulties in their life's journey. Once the client has clarity concerning the issue, they can then be helped to challenge and overcome that which has been feeding into their psychological and emotional distress, which may have led to anxiety, depression, or negative self-perception.

Solution-focused (SFT) therapists often work creatively with their clients by adopting the Miracle Question strategy (de Shazer, 1985/1988). The Miracle Question help the client explore what their life would be like if a particular problem did not exist. This question is usually phrased like, 'If you woke up tomorrow morning and a miracle had happened and you no longer felt depressed (or whatever the emotion resulting from their issue/s), what would be different?' This exercise aims to provide a starting point to help the client become motivated to bring about change.

A pluralistic therapist will most likely be open to a creative way of working with clients; McLeod stated, "Even when drawing on established and well-understood therapy ideas and methods, both client and therapist strive to achieve moments of creativity when something new, some shift in perception of feeling that fits and seems right, emerges and becomes apparent" (McLeod, 2018, p. 3). Establishing an environment that fosters moments of creativity can enable the therapist to offer a creative approach for the client to consider. An example of this in my practice was when a client talked about a family photograph she visualised in her mind and began exploring her sense of aloneness within the family structure. I invited her to consider working with that photograph in more depth to explore her loneliness. She was interested in working this way and explored the photograph in her own time outside the session. She brought her experience of working with this photograph to the following session, where she communicated painful memories from her childhood. In her feedback at the end of therapy, this was one of the most meaningful aspects of her therapy, as she informed me that the creative aspect helped her voice her feelings regarding her childhood and that validating her hurt in the therapy sessions was essential to her recovery.

When adapting methods from various therapeutic approaches in pluralistic therapy, "a collaborative, dialogical stance" (McLeod & Sundet, 2016, p. 167) is essential (Cooper & McLeod, 2011). Shared decision-making, where the therapist asks dialogical questions to facilitate two-way communication and encourage deeper reflection (McLeod, 2018), is required. One example is for the client and therapist to consider a relaxation technique for anxiety, often used in CBT (Geeanjali et al., 2023).

Geetanjal et al.'s (2023) review paper concludes how "mindfulness-based practices, CBT, physical activity and relaxation methods can lower stress levels and enhance mental health in general" (p 347). Once agreed through collaboration, further reflection on this relaxation strategy could be done before and after the client practises this method as "a commitment to transparency and shared decision-making" (McLeod, 2018, p. 1) and to assess its usefulness for that specific client, which could be relevant for future work.

In comparison with single modalities such as PCT, CBT, SFT, and Psychodynamic approaches, the pluralistic stance assumes "that different things are likely to help different people at different points in time" (Cooper & McLeod, 2011, p. 6). Therefore, the attitude that there is one best theoretical approach is not conducive to a pluralistic stance. The pluralistic assumption that it is beneficial to work collaboratively with clients to "decide on the focus and course of therapy" (Cooper & McLeod, 2011, p. 6) leverages the strengths of both the client and the therapist. Furthermore, the therapist can share their knowledge to offer ideas that the client might want to consider. McLeod (2018) suggests that pluralistic therapists will always be agreeable when a client enquires or suggests a particular way of working. For example, if a client wants to explore a dream and discuss how to approach it, this would involve shared decision-making. However, sometimes a client may ask the therapist for guidance, so in order to be collaborative, it would be necessary to frame any suggestion as 'trying out' a new idea or technique to see whether it might be helpful for the client" (McLeod, 2018, p. 117), maintaining collaboration.

In my professional experience, the majority of clients enthusiastically engage in discussions about working creatively, and many are eager to try out a different approach to exploring their issues. Dryden (Cooper & Dryden, 2016) invites anxious clients to consider their anxiety to be like a plant (pp. 188–189). Dryden explains how the plant metaphor helps a client to explore what it is that causes their "anxiety to thrive and "what would cause it to wither" (p. 188). Such insight can be a powerful motivator for change.

When a client is considering whether to try working creatively, McLeod (2018) suggests that the therapist facilitates collaborative dialogue, which he described as 'metacommunication'. This involves responding to the intentions and reactions of both the client and the therapist (p. 83). This purposeful dialogue (McLeod, 2018) can involve the therapist asking Socratic questions (Padesky, 1993), thereby contributing to the purposeful dialogue. Padesky suggested that a good Socratic question helps in the guided discovery of what the client "doesn't say" and helps them move "from the concrete to the abstract" (Padesky, 1993, p. 2). Kennerley (2007, p. 23) provides examples of a therapist asking Socratic questions, including "What can you see in your mind's eye?" and "Can you tell me more about what's happening for you right now?".

Regarding the practice of drawing on different methods, the question might be asked, 'How is the pluralistic approach different from an integrative or an eclectic approach?' McLeod and Sundet (2016) describe the eclectic approach as "drawing on a wide repertoire of skills and ideas" (p. 159) depending on what is best for that client at that time. Similarly, an integrative approach will also share a willingness to incorporate techniques and theories in therapy (McLeod & Sundet, 2016, p. 160). However, this could be done in a "therapist-directed way, without ever consulting the client on what they want or varying it for different clients" (Cooper & McLeod, July 15, 2019. https://pluralisticpractice.com/. Retrieved 16 October 2024).

Assimilative integration is a form of integration that involves a therapist who is trained in one approach and, through their continued practice with clients, "gradually incorporate them into their client work" (McLeod & Sundet, 2016, p. 160), developing their integrative style of therapy. However, the main difference regarding pluralistic therapy is that "it is less focused on combining techniques and theories, and more focused on being flexible and adaptable to the individual needs of each client" (Blunden, 2022, https://pluralisticpractice.com/. Retrieved 16 October 2024). Through collaboration, the therapist engages in a dialogical conversation to establish the approach which works best for the client. This collaborative process is central to pluralistic therapy, valuing and prizing differences, and ensuring that, as therapists, we hold the client's autonomy and contribution to the decision-making process as central to the therapeutic process.

When working creatively, therapists can offer structured or unstructured creative interventions depending on the client's preference. For a structured intervention, guidance is given to help a client engage with the creative process when they need support to begin the process, and such guidance can be verbal or in the form of a written handout. In comparison, an example of an unstructured intervention may involve the client drawing or painting an emotion relating to an issue. Then, once they have completed their image, they can engage in free writing. This part of the process could involve focusing on the image, and then when they feel moved to express their thoughts and feelings regarding their creative output, they can begin writing in an experiential way. Clients who prefer not to write could record verbal reflections on their images. The creative output and reflections produced by the client would then be unpacked further in a therapy session.

A development within the field of counselling and psychotherapy is the emergence of online therapy, which is becoming an increasingly popular method of delivering therapy by many professionals. The coronavirus disease (COVID-19) resulted in a pandemic, and physical distancing measures, including government-mandated lockdowns, were implemented in 2020 (Liu et al., 2021). Such restrictions on person-to-person contact made face-to-face therapy problematic; therefore, online therapies substantially increased (Giordano et al., 2022).

From a personal perspective, my experience aligns with Giordano et al. (2022). During the pandemic, I had to adjust my approach from face-to-face therapy to delivering therapy online. However, this approach has become the predominant method of delivering therapy to my clients. I have adapted the creative interventions I delivered during face-to-face client work to working creatively online. Throughout this book, working creatively in online therapy can be as effective as face-to-face creative therapy, and each intervention presented will be considered for its application in both online and face-to-face settings.

For online therapy, it is essential to use a secure platform. Many online organisations already have this set up for therapists listed with them, ensuring confidentiality and privacy. For example, the organisation I am registered with has a secure platform that enables me to send messages and attachments to the client. Today, it is common for clients to use an iPhone, allowing them to upload a photograph of any creative output so that it can be referred to during a session.

Regarding the diversity and cultural backgrounds of clients, including ethnicity, religion, gender, age, disability, and socioeconomic status, it is essential to stay alongside the client in understanding their interpretation of a symbol or metaphor. Certain groups share a common interpretation of a symbol, while for others, an individual meaning is most significant. I advise a therapist to 'let the client tell you their meaning'. Empathy regarding the issue of diversity is crucial when working creatively with clients.

References

Bandura, A. (1997). *Self-efficacy: The exercise of control*. Freeman.

Blunden, N. (2022). https://pluralisticpractice.com/. Retrieved 16 October 2024.

Coolidge, F. L., Lavie, P., & Blenkinsopp, A. (2006). *Dream interpretation as a psychotherapeutic technique*. Radcliffe Publishing.

Cooper, M. (2007). Humanizing psychotherapy. *Journal of Contemporary Psychotherapy, 37*(1), 11–16.

Cooper, M., & McLeod, J. (2007). A pluralistic framework for counselling and psychotherapy: Implications for research. *Counselling and Psychotherapy Research, 7*(3), 135–143. http://eprints.edlr.strath.ac.uk/s213/

Cooper, M., & McLeod, J. (2011). *Pluralistic counselling and psychotherapy*. London: Sage.

Cooper, M., Mearns, D., Stiles, W. B., Warren, M., & Elliott, R. (2004). Developing self-pluralistic perspectives and experiential approaches: A round-table dialogue. *Person-Centered and Experiential Psychotherapies, 3*(3), 176–191.

de Shazer, S. (1985). *Keys to solution in brief therapy*. New York: W. W. Norton & Company.

de Shazer, S. (1988). *Clues: Investigating solution in brief therapy*. New York. W. W. Norton & Company.

Dollinger, S. J., Urban, K. K., & James, T. J. (2004). Creativity and openness: Further validation of two creative product measures. *Creativity Research Journal, 16*, 35–48.

Dryden, W. (2016). Helping client address problematic anxiety. In M. Cooper & W. Dryden (Eds.), *The handbook of pluralistic counselling and psychotherapy* (Chapter 15, pp. 173–183). Sage.

Fisher, B. J., & Specht, D. K. (1999). Successful aging and creativity in later life. *Journal of Aging Studies, 13*(4), 457–472.

Fleet, D. (2019). *Transformation hidden in the sand: Developing a theoretical frame-work using a sand-tray interventions with adult clients* (Doctoral thesis, Staffordshire University). Stoke-on-Trent. Available from Ethos STORE – Staffordshire Online Repository. http://eprints.staffs.ac.uk/id/eprnt/5763

Fleet, D. (2023). *Pluralistic sand-tray therapy – Humanistic principles for working creatively with adult clients.* Routledge: Taylor & Francis Group.

Fleet, D., Reeves, A., Burton, A., & DasGupta, M. P. (2021). Transformation hidden in the sand: A pluralistic theoretical framework using sand-tray with adult clients. First published online (14 June 2021). *Journal of Creativity in Mental Health.* https://doi.org/10.1080/15401383.2021.1936738

Freud, S. (1900). *The interpretation of dreams* (T. Griffith, Ed.; A. A. Brill. Trans.; Wordsworth class edition). Wordsworth Editions.

Freud, S. (1924). *A general introduction to psychoanalysis* (J. Riviere, Trans.).

Geeanjali, A., Wahane, S., & Sharma, A. (2023). Exploring effective strategies for stress management: Enhancing mental well-being through mindfulness, CBT, exercise, and relaxation techniques. *Bulletin of Environment, Pharmacology and Life Sciences, 12*(5), 345–348. ©2023 Academy for Environment and Life Sciences, India. Online ISSN 2277-1808. http://www.bepls.com CODEN:BEPLAD

Gendlin, E. T. (1996). *Focusing orientated psychotherapy.* New York: Guildford Press.

Giordano, C., Amrosiano, I., Graffeo, M. T., DiCaro, A., & Gullo S. (2022, December 29). The transition to online psychotherapy during the pandemic: A qualitative study on patients' perspectives. *Research Psychotherapy, 25*(3), 638. Published online 2022 November 4. https://doi.org/10.4081/ripppo.2022.638

Greenberg, L. S. (2004). Being and doing: Person-centeredness, process guidance and different treatment. *Person-Centered & Experiential Psychotherapies, 3*(1), 52–64.

Gruber, H. E., & Davis, S. N. (1988). Inching our way up Mount Olympus. The evolving-systems approach to creative thinking. In R. J. Sternberg (Ed.), *The nature of creativity* (pp. 243–270). New York: Cambridge University Press.

Hawker, S. (2006). *The little Oxford dictionary* (9th ed.). Oxford University Press.

Hefferon, K., Grealy, M., & Mutrie, N. (2010). Transforming from cocoon to butterfly: The potential role of the body in the process of posttraumatic

growth. *Journal of Humanistic Psychology, 50*(2), 224–247. http://www.sagepub.com/journalsPermissions.nav. https://doi.org/10.1177/0022167809341996. http://jhp.sagepub.com
Jung, C. G. (1959). *The concept of the collective unconscious* (R. F. C. Hull, Trans. In: Part I: Archetypes and the collective unconscious, Vol.9. Princeton University Press. (Original work published 1936).
Jung, C. G. (1972). *Mandala symbolism.* Princeton University Press.
Jung, C. G. (1974). *Dreams* (R. F. C. Hull, Trans.; 2nd ed.). Routledge.
Kalff, D. M. (1980). *Sandplay*. Sigo Press.
Kennerley, H. (2007). *Socratic method*. Oxford Cognitive Therapy Centre, Warneford Hospital.
Killick, S., Curry, V., & Myles, P. (2016). The mighty metaphor: A collection of therapists' favourite metaphors and analogies. *The Cognitive Behaviour Therapist, 9*, e37, 1–13. https://doi.org/10.1017/S1754470X16000210
Liu, C. Y., Berlin, J., Moses, C., Kiti, C., Del Fava, E., Grow, A., Zagheni, E., Melegaro, A., Jenness, S. M., Omer, S. B., Lopman, B., & Nelson, K. (2021, November). Rapid review of social contact patterns during the COVID-19 pandemic. *Epidemiology, 32*(6), 781–791. https://doi.org/10.1097/EDE.0000000000001412
Malchiodi, C. (2005). *Expressive therapies*. The Guildford Press.
Maslow, A. H. (1971). *The farther reaches of human nature*. Viking.
May, R. (1994). *The courage to create.* Norton (Originally published in 1975).
May, R. (1996). *The meaning of anxiety*. Norton (Originally published in 1950).
McLeod, J. (2018). *Pluralistic therapy. Distinctive features*. Routledge. Taylor & Francis Group.
McLeod, J., & Sundet, R. (2016). *The handbook of pluralistic counselling and psychotherapy* (M. Cooper & W. Dryden, Eds., p. 167, Chapter 13). Sage.
Mearns, D., & Thorne, B. (2000). *Person-centred therapy today.* Sage Publications Ltd.
Padesky, C. (1993). *Socratic questioning: Changing minds or guiding discovery?* ECBT Keynote Address: London.
Perls, F. (1969). *Gestalt therapy verbatim*. Bantam.
Polanyi, M. (1958; 1998). *Personal knowledge: Towards a post-critical philosophy*. Routledge.
Rogers, C. R. (1957). The necessary and sufficient conditions of therapeutic personality change. *Journal of Consulting Psychology, 21*, 95–103.
Rogers, C. R. (1961). *On becoming a person.* Houghton Mifflin.

Rogers, C. R. (1995). *On becoming a person: A therapist's view of psychotherapy*. Houghton Mifflin (Original work published in 1969).

Rogers, N. (2000). *The creative connection: Expressive arts as healing*. PCCS Books.

Rogers, N., Tudor, K., Embleton Tudor, L., & Keemar, K. (2012). Person-centered expressive arts therapy: A theoretical encounter. *Person-Centered & Experiential Psychotherapies, 11*(1), 31–47.

Runco, M. A. (2014). *Creativity – theories and themes: Research development and practice* (2nd ed.). Elsevier.

Silverstone, L. (1997). *Art therapy – the person-centred way: Art and the development of the person* (2nd ed.). Jessica Kingsley Publishers.

Stoddard, J. A., & Afari, N. (2014). *The big book of ACT metaphors: A practitioner's guide to experiential exercise & metaphors in acceptance and commitment therapy.* New Harbinger Publications Inc.

Taylor, J. (1992). *Where people fly and water runs uphill: Using dreams to tap the wisdom of the unconscious*. Warner.

Thomas, V. (2016). *Using mental imagery in counselling and psychotherapy: A guide to more inclusive theory and practice*. Routledge.

Torrance, E. P., Clements, C. B., & Geoff, K. (1989). Mind-body learning among the elderly: Arts, fitness incubation. *Educational Forum, 54*, 123–133.

Turner, B. A. (2005). *The handbook of sandplay therapy*. Temenos Press.

Whitfield, C. L. (1987). *Healing the child within: Discovery and recovery for adult children of dysfunctional families.* Health Communications Inc.

2

Working with Images

Arthur Brisbane is recognised as the first person to use the quote, "*A picture is worth a thousand words*" (Brisbane, 1911, p. 18). I believe this quote encapsulates the power of using images in creative therapy as sometimes, an image can convey more meaning than words alone. Furthermore, Comfort (1985) suggested that introducing clients to the visual language of images is of real value in the therapeutic relationship as this method helps them talk about experiences that are otherwise difficult to speak of. In addition, a client may have a sense of something but be unable to find the words to describe it accurately; creative exploration of that implicit experience can help them engage in edge of awareness (Gendlin, 1996) discovery. Using images can result in a more explicit understanding, with them finding the words that fit. Furthermore, the symbols in an image can help access experience from the unconscious; this material, which was initially entirely out of awareness, can then be processed consciously with the help of a therapist.

Comfort (1985) suggests that published pictures can be powerful tools for evoking complex emotions and relationships in therapy. I support this approach and have used similar images in my clinical practice. Clients often find them intriguing and engaging, helping them to become

D. Fleet, *Creative Interventions in Counselling and Psychotherapy*, Palgrave Texts in Counselling and Psychotherapy, https://doi.org/10.1007/978-3-032-16609-8_2

motivated to explore the meaning of the symbols and make personal connections from their chosen image.

Library of Images

In my practice, I provide clients who have expressed an interest in such creative work using my diverse library of images. These images can be sourced from a variety of places, including greeting cards, photographs. and computer-based pictures. They are then laminated to ensure durability, allowing for continuous handling by clients.

For example, several clients chose an image depicting a small person sitting on an oversized chair, with their feet unable to touch the floor (Image 2.1).

To help with diversity, I have taken the same photograph, including people of different genders, ethnic background and body types.

In my work with clients who have selected this image to explore their distress, emerging issues have included feelings of 'stuckness', insecurity, insignificance, disrespect, imposter syndrome, not feeling good enough, and not being acknowledged, validated or respected. The image has been significant in the therapeutic process by facilitating deeper exploration and helping the clients to express their feelings, enabling their voices to be heard and bringing change, such as an increase in their self-esteem and self-confidence. In addition, processing past and present painful experiences can lead clients to actively bring change for a brighter future.

Working with this image, some helpful, purposeful questions I have asked to aid the client engage in deeper reflection and process unresolved issues include:

'Who is that sitting on that chair?'
'What experiences come up for you sitting on that huge chair?'
'If the chair had a voice, what might it say to you?'
'What would you like to say to that chair?'
'Can you jump off that chair?'
'Did you climb on that chair yourself?'

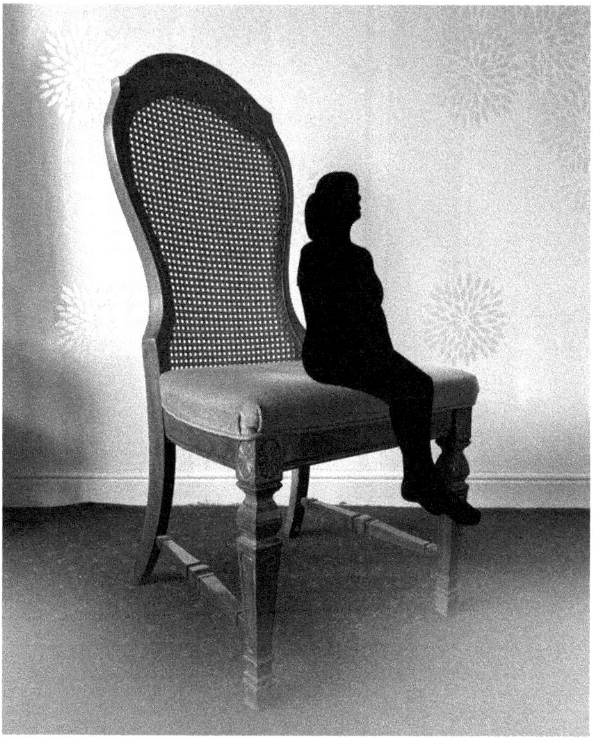

Image 2.1 Small person sitting on an oversized chair

Case Study: Tanya

Tanya was an online client who had a propensity for working creatively which was established in a purposeful discussion in the initial session. One of her goals was to explore a toxic relationship, with the task of sharing the painful impact on her. I offered her the method of working with images, and after a two-way dialogue, she was happy to do so. Her chosen image was a photograph of the washing of hands (Image 2.2).

The picture shows hands cupped together, palms facing up, and water pouring into them. We decided that Tanya would work with the image before the next session. I suggested that she find some private space where she would not be disturbed and begin by practising the breathing strategy to help her prepare herself to engage with the process. Then, look at the

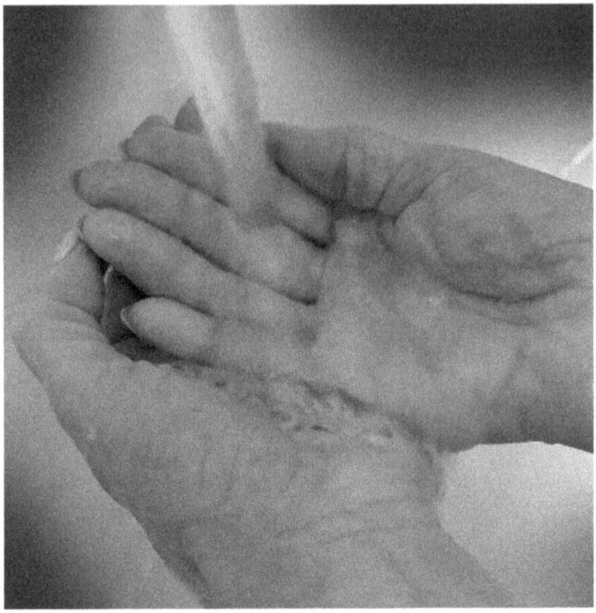

Image 2.2 Washing of hands

image for 10 minutes and immerse herself in free writing, writing down any thoughts or feelings that came up for her without editing.

The following quotations are part of Tanya's reflection, which she entitled:

> "A picture speaks a thousand words":
>
> > "The picture describes the internal process I'm going through right now…just as one washes the dirt off one's hands and feels clean thereafter, I am feeling the weight of many unnecessary components in my life, melting away and making way for the new. The process of letting certain people go was painful and unpleasant in the beginning.
> > However, I no longer see the point in dedicating time, energy, and resources to people who are unreliable, reactive, uncaring, and downright unpleasant. I also find myself currently in the process of

> myself washing my hands of the old image of myself I carried
> around
> i.e. chaotic, messy, unstable, insecure, depressive, sick, weak, unre-
> liable
> and so on. I am working towards being the version of myself I want
> to
> be. The new me is strong, healthy, happy, confident, smart, kind,
> creative,
> and resilient. The new me is not scared to speak her mind once
> again".

Tanya had a difficult childhood, as one member of her family was consistently emotionally and psychologically abusive. The expectations placed upon her were extraordinarily high, and something was only good enough if it was exceptional. The benefit of such high expectations was that Tanya became a gifted child and later a gifted adult, with her achievements recognised by others. However, there was a high price to pay, as Tanya began to take on the self-perception that she was never good enough, culminating in developing a strong Inner Critic and a perfectionist attitude. Often, the origin of an Inner Critic can be established in childhood by significant others frequently judging the child (Early & Weiss, 2013). A child often criticised for failing to meet the impossibly high expectations set by significant others can develop a strong inner critic.

With Tanya, this continued effort to push herself to do better and attempt perfection was emotionally exhausting. Eventually, during therapy, in her quest for happiness, she decided to cut this person out of her life, and although this was a painful decision for her to make due to family resistance, she saw it as her having no other option if she wanted to bring change.

Case Study Bee

Bee was another online client who worked with the 'washing of hands' image in between sessions. This variation in symbolism between the two clients is a good example of how working with an image will have individual meaning for each person. Therefore, it is important for the therapist to avoid making assumptions about the meaning of an image and stay close to the client's interpretation so that the therapist remains in the client's frame of reference.

Bee's presenting problem was one of abandonment, as her partner had ended their relationship without giving her a solid reason why. Bee was confused, as they had both shared that they loved each other and wanted to be exclusive in their relationship. However, at this time, Bee still loved him and wanted him to return to her. Even though Bee was hurt, she found the loss of her relationship hard to accept. We began to explore her ex-partner's behaviour since ending the relationship, and she began to acknowledge how this was unacceptable, stating "he went from hot to cold", but at this time, she still yearned for him to return to her. In the session, following her creative discovery, using the image she shared:

> 'The water is running into and through my hands. Why am I trying to hold onto it? The water does not want to be held! The water is him…. I'm done!'

These realisations had a profound impact on Bee, bringing a phenomenological shift (Fleet, 2019, 2023, p. 38; Fleet et al., 2021) involving a change in her emotions and in her perception of her ex-partner. Furthermore, another person had informed her that her ex-partner was now seeing another woman, and she began to feel angry, which she was able to express. This information motivated her to see things differently and realise that his uncaring attitude was disrespectful and that she deserved much more than he could give. She was then able to think about a future without him.

A further example taken from my library of images and used in my practice relates to an image of a young girl around 7 years old holding the hand of a younger boy around 4 years old and in her other hand, she carries an empty shopping bag. This photograph represented the client's experience of the heavy expectations placed upon her by her parents of being responsible for looking after her younger brother and having to do tasks rather than play with the other children. Using the image, a missed childhood was explored by the client, bringing up feelings of loss and being forced to act older than her years. Furthermore, this photograph was the trigger to explore other experiences related to feelings of loss about her 'missing' childhood, and Inner Child (Capacchione, 1991) work was discussed as a method for her to explore her unresolved pain.

Capacchione (1991) stated how the Inner Child is an aspect of the Self, which "is a powerful presence"(p. 16) and "for us to be fully human, the Child Within must be embraced and expressed" (p. 17). However, experiencing childhood abuse, including physical, psychological and emotional abuse, as well as abandonment and neglect, can result in a wounded Inner Child, which can have a long-lasting painful influence due to old distress as an adult (Bradshaw, 1990). Bradshaw (1990) suggested that engaging in this type of therapeutic work could bring rapid relief as it involves change at such depth, and past wounds can be healed (1990).

Salma was happy to engage in this work, and we decided how the method of writing a letter to her Inner Child, taking a compassionate approach, might be useful to help her meet the task of processing her past issues that still had an impact on her. She began by asking her Inner Child, 'What do you want to tell me?' This question was the springboard to her connecting with her inner Child, and the work continued for several weeks. She began offering genuine compassion and understanding to this aspect of self, which was a significant part of her healing process. After several weeks, she had a photograph of her as a young girl framed and placed in a prominent position in her home to remind her to keep offering compassion to that aspect of herself.

Another image chosen by several clients is a photograph of a street artist's drawing of an enormous baby, sitting in a hole in the road, being fed with a giant spoon by a tiny adult. This powerful image has represented many different things to different clients and as the therapist; I guide each client to interpret the image in their own way, empowering them to take control in their search for understanding.

However, this illustration has often represented a problematic relationship, with no balance between 'give and take'. Here, the client commonly associates with the adult continuously feeding (giving to) the baby (the other person). Continuous egocentricity displayed by a partner can lead to resentment, anger, and conflict. Some clients can find themselves in a co-dependent relationship with them, often trapped into enabling the other's abusive behaviour, resulting in anxiety, and diminishing self-esteem. Cermak (1986) suggested that codependency is a dysfunctional pattern of relating to others regarding personality and behaviour. Such behaviour can involve one individual focusing on their partner's needs detrimental to their own, and that person may get to the point of self-abandonment, resulting in low self-esteem. Furthermore, the individual with low self-esteem may find it immensely difficult to end the relationship due to a lack of self-confidence as a barrier to them leaving.

However, suppose the client decides they want to stay in this problematic relationship but to bring an element of change. In that case, a review of their boundaries is often needed, involving those limits and rules we set ourselves in relationships, which are reworked as they begin to realise they also have needs to be met. Such realisation can help the client to acknowledge how self-respect and respect for each other are essential to building a healthy relationship. However, suppose there is no opportunity for change, blocking a move to establish more give-and-take in their relationship. This realisation can often result in a breakdown. Then, the client must consider whether to stay in this unsatisfactory relationship or leave, which can be explored in therapy.

Phototherapy

Questioning Brisbane's quote, "A picture is worth a thousand words" (Brisbane, 1911, p. 18), Gibson's (2017) response was, "It depends on how it is used" (Gibson, 2017, p. 46). Photographs can be a valuable resource for clients in therapy, but the therapist needs to have the knowledge to aid the therapeutic process, benefiting the client. Weiser (1984, 2001, 2004) distinguishes between phototherapy, which requires a trained counsellor/therapist to offer structured use of photographs, and therapeutic photography, which can be self-initiated, either individually or in a group, not requiring a formally trained therapist.

Moreover, Lowenthal (2023) suggested how working with a client's personal photographs "can be used in ordinary counselling, psychotherapy and psychoanalysis" (p. 2). Asiret and Kapucu (2015) reinforce this way of working and argue how photographs of earlier times can help clients explore their thoughts and feelings related to their past.

Lowenthal (2023) supported this stance (2023) and suggested how this reminiscence approach is the most common way to work with photographs in therapy. Stewart (1979) was specific in the benefits this method can offer as it reduces or relieves "painful psychological symptoms" and can facilitate "psychological growth and change" (p. 41). Similarly, Weiser (2004) stated how "personal snapshots and family photos (and the feelings, memories, thoughts and information they evoke)…can be used by any kind of trained therapist regardless of conceptual orientation…" (p. 23). Weiser adds, "Photographs *always* tell stories" (Weiser, 2004, p. 23) especially when words alone are not enough.

Therapeutic Examples

I have often worked with online and face-to-face clients who wanted to use personal photographs in the therapeutic process. I suggest that they find photographs of themselves at various ages. For example, this could be ages 5, 10, 16, and their current age and working with each photograph in turn to look at the photograph and explore the purposeful questions below:

1. How would you describe yourself at that age?
2. What emotions/feelings come up for you when you look at that aspect of you?
3. If that aspect of you had a voice, what would they say to you?
4. What did they need then? (*Here the reader may sense a shift in focus from 'you' to 'them'. This is purposeful to help the client engage with that aspect of self, helping them process from the observer-experiencer position*).
5. What do you want to tell them?
6. Do they have any dreams for the future?
7. What made them: happy, sad, excited, angry, scared?

8. What are your feelings towards them?
9. What can you learn from them…from you at that age?

This photograph strategy works well with online and face-to-face clients, as they work on this activity during the week prior to therapy session. Then sharing their reflections in the therapy session allows validation of their insights and edge of awareness exploration, bringing further insight.

I have had clients send me their photographs on my secure online platform, while others have held the photograph up to the screen while talking through their reflections. Whatever is the best option for the client, I am happy to accommodate, as their sense of autonomy is the priority.

The benefits from this work include helping the client work through the impact of past experience and unresolved distress, including relationships that had a detrimental and even traumatic impact on the client, which need processing.

In addition, past activities that brought joy to them when younger can be considered, exploring the possibility that such activities can be reintroduced into their lives in some way that may bring a sense of joy once again, even in a minimised capacity. For example, past clients who loved to dance as children have taken up dance classes as adults, clients who loved teachers or parents reading to them as children have joined reading clubs where they can share ideas and some clients who loved to write stories as children have engaged in journal writing, poetry, with some even writing their life story.

However, some clients do not have childhood photographs, yet they can still benefit from using photographs in therapy. For example, they can create an album by taking symbolic photographs that may represent past experiences. For instance, a photograph of a young sapling with broken branches may represent an abusive childhood. The symbolism can be powerful, and the therapist can help the client connect with that symbol on a personal level, helping them explore and express unresolved emotions. A photograph of a tiger taken at the Zoo may symbolise the client's inner strength that got them through a difficult situation, such as standing up to a bully as a teenager, learning to say no or simply existing now and being in therapy after a traumatised past.

Lowenthal (2023) shares his experience of therapeutic photography when he was suffering from exhaustion and depression while on holiday with his family. Three of the photographs he took he named 'The blues 1', 'The blues 2' and 'The blues 3' (Lowenthal, 2023, p. 31) which were gloomy images. The other photographs were of his family members looking happy (Lowenthal, 2023, pp. 31–33). These photographs enabled him "to come to terms with" his depression and exhaustion "and work through it" (Lowenthal, 2023, p. 33) bringing a positive shift in his emotional and psychological state. Lowenthal (2023) cites Craig (2009) who argued how such photography helps the individual to see things from a different perspective and facilitates reflection, communication, and expression that go "beyond words" (Lowenthal, 2023, p. 39).

Using images in therapy is an adaptable, creative intervention that can be used in face-to-face or online work. In my experience, it is more effective for the client to work on the image on their own in between sessions so that they have the time to engage in deep reflection and then bring their insights and creative output for unpacking in the next therapy session. In addition, the client's autonomous process is a central feature as they work independently outside of therapy and then their reflections are explored and validated in the following therapy session.

Taking a different perspective, images can occur when a client is experiencing intrusive images due to either trauma or a perceived threatening situation visualising a terrifying situation that might occur, the client may be highly distressed, and a therapist needs to offer a strategy to manage that.

Cast Study Freda

I was working with Freda, who had an intrusive image of the face of her elderly mother, who had just died as Freda walked into the hospital room for that final visit. Freda described how what she saw did not look like her mother and she was very distressed. Each night, while trying to get to sleep, this disturbing image would come into her mind, and she would experience the distressing emotions associated with it. We discussed the possible methods to work with this image, and she was happy to work on transforming this distressing image into a more benign one. Holmes et al. (2007) describe how imagery techniques involving transforming an existing negative mental image into a more benign image can be effective for distressed clients. After preparing to try this strategy in the therapy session, the following night, when the image came into her mind, Freda imagined it was pixilating, turning into a happy, and smiling photograph of her mother taken the Christmas before when she was well. It did take practice, and even after the first few times of practice, she stated she felt she was slowly gaining control, and after a few weeks, the intrusion of that image at night began to dissipate completely. We also discussed how Freda could frame that happy photograph and place it in her lounge at home, which she did to remind her to keep visualising this positive image of her mother.

In summary, freely available images from various sources and photographs can be used as powerful therapeutic tools for evoking complex emotions in therapy. Such images can be used in a variety of ways, depending on the client's preference. Suppose the therapist wants to take a pluralistic approach. In that case, it is helpful to consider possible purposeful questions to ask the client about the image they have chosen, in addition to the usual counselling skills such as reflecting, paraphrasing and summarising.

References

Asiret, G., & Kapucu, S. (2015). The effect of reminiscence therapy on cognition, depression, and activities of daily living for patients with Alzheimer disease. *Journal of Geriatric Psychiatry and Neurology, 29*(1), 31–37.

Bradshaw, J. (1990). *Home coming. Reclaiming & championing your inner child*. Bantam Books. ISBN 0-7499-1054-2.

Brisbane, A. (1911, April 20). Newspaper copy that people must read, advertising's relation to the growth of reading ability—The thunderstorm and "yellow" journalism—An example of the power of comparison in writing. *Printers' Ink, A Journal for Advertisers*, 17.

Capacchione, L. (1991). *Recovery of your inner child*. Simon & Schuster.

Cermak, T. L. (1986). Diagnostic criteria for codependency. *Journal of Psychoactive Drugs, 18*(1), 15–20. https://doi.org/10.1080/02791072.1986.10524475

Comfort, C. E. (1985). Published pictures of psychotherapeutic tools. *Arts in Psychotherapy., 12*(4), 245–256.
Craig, C. (2009). *Explorig the self in photography.* Hatchett. https://blog-deposit-photos.com/therapeutic-photographs.html
Earley, J., & Weiss, B. (2013). *Freedom from your inner critic. A self-therapy approach.* Sounds True Inc.
Fleet, D. (2019). *Transformation hidden in the sand: Developing a theoretical frame-work using a sand-tray interventions with adult clients* (Doctoral thesis, Staffordshire University). Stoke-on-Trent. Available from Ethos STORE – Staffordshire Online Repository. http://eprints.staffs.ac.uk/id/eprnt/5763
Fleet, D. (2023). *Pluralistic sand-tray therapy – Humanistic principles for working creatively with adult clients.* Routledge: Taylor & Francis Group.
Fleet, D., Reeves, A., Burton, A., & DasGupta, M. P. (2021). Transformation hidden in the sand: A pluralistic theoretical framework using sand-tray with adult clients. First published online (14 June 2021). *Journal of Creativity in Mental Health.* https://doi.org/10.1080/15401383.2021.1936738
Gendlin, E. T. (1984). The client's client: The edge of awareness. In R. L. Levant & J.M. Shlien (Eds.), *Client-centered therapy and the person-centered approach. New directions in theory, research and practice.* Praeger.
Gendlin, E. T. (1996). Focusing orientated psychotherapy. New York: Guildford Press.
Gibson, N. (2017, January). Therapeutic photography: Enhancing patient communication. *Kidney Care, 2*(1). https://www.magonlinelibrary.com/doi/epub/10.12968/jokc.2017.2.1.46. Retrieved 5 September 2024.
Holmes, E. A., Arntz, A., & Smucker, M. R. (2007). Imagery rescripting in cognitive behaviour therapy: Images, treatment techniques and outcomes. *Journal of Behavior Therapy and Experimental Psychiatry, 38*, 297–305. https://doi.org/10.1016/j.jbtep.2007.10.007
Lowenthal, D. (2023). *The handbook of phototherapy and therapeutic photography, for the professional and activist client.* Routledge. Taylor & Francis Group.
Stewart, D. (1979). *Photo therapy: Theory and practice. Art Psychotherapy*, 6, 41–46. https://doi.org/10.1016/0090-9092(79)90019-X
Weiser, J. (1984). Phototherapy–becoming visually literate about oneself, or, phototherapy?? What's phototherapy?? *Phototherapy, 4*(2), 2–7.
Weiser, J. (2001). Phototherapy techniques: Using clients' personal snapshots and family photos as counseling and therapy tools. *Afterimage, 29*(3), 10–15.

Weiser, J. (2004). PhotoTherapy techniques in counseling and therapy: Using ordinary snapshots and photo-interactions to help clients heal their lives. *Canadian art Therapy Association Journal, 17*(2), 23–53.

3
Mandala Art Therapy

Henderson et al. (2007) define a mandala "as a meditative tool in various religions" but it is more commonly known in Tibetan Buddhism as involving "a circular design that is thought to promote psychological healing and integration" (p. 149). For Jung (1972), the mandala is about deep meaning, the realisation of inner experience often chaotic and marked by conflict, with mandala therapy having the potential to bring reconciliation and wholeness (pp. 99–100).

Carl Jung (1875–1961), a voracious academic publisher of his work exploring the human psyche, with many texts published posthumously by editors after his death, is widely acknowledged as the first professional to use mandala art in therapy with his patients. Jung (Illing, 1963) gradually discovered the therapeutic benefits of mandala art after regularly engaging in circular drawings of his intra-psychic experience. The circle shape of the mandala is a protected space with the author illustrating their conscious and unconscious experience linked to their inner conflict and distress (Jung, 1973; Kostyunina & Drozdikova-Zaripova, 2016) with the material in art form available for self-expression. The shape of the circle has powerful symbolism, occurring in many different religions and cultures and is significant in mandala art therapy. Glen

D. Fleet, *Creative Interventions in Counselling and Psychotherapy*, Palgrave Texts in Counselling and Psychotherapy, https://doi.org/10.1007/978-3-032-16609-8_3

Rogers suggests "how the circle is the archetypal symbol of wholeness and unity" (Glen Rogers, 2018). It "has no corners to become over-stressed and break", having "no beginning and no end", and "distributes weight across its entire surface with an even balance" (Simmons, 2001, p. 14).

The wholeness of the circle is central to the ancient Chinese yin-yang symbol representing life, which has "two opposing forces" within the circle "that are constantly trying to gain the upper hand, but neither will succeed" (Jaeger, www.intechopen.com. Retrieved 2 January 2025, p. 31).

For example, opposites include "masculinity and femininity, large and small, heaven and earth" (Xinyan, 2013, p. 77), yet they are viewed as interconnected and complementary, as depicted in the Yin-Yang symbol. The minor black spot in the white section and the minor white spot in the black section illustrate "how both Yin and Yang carry the seed of their opposites" (Jaeger. www.intechopen.com. Retrieved 2 January 2025, p. 26). The "constant struggle between opposites…produces the rhythm of life (Jaeger, 2025, p. 30).

Such contradictions and paradoxes are interdependent, representing a way of life in Chinese culture (Fang, 2012; King & Zhang, 2014).

Similarly, working with his inner conflict using mandala art, Jung came to realise "the wholeness of the personality" (pp. 195–196) with inner conflict being potentially harmonious, with potential benefits for his patients in therapy.

Following on from Jung's work on mandala art therapy, this creative method is being increasingly adopted by various mental health professionals to help people explore their thoughts and feelings (Babouchkina & Robbins, 2015; Kim et al., 2018). Pisarik and Larson (2011) suggested how mandala art therapy had positive psychological effects, increasing the subjective well-being of college students. Kim et al. (2018) also suggested benefits in how mandala art therapy increased hope in psychiatric inpatients. Furthermore, Henderson et al. (2007) argued how mandala art therapy has the capacity to decrease symptoms related to trauma in individuals.

Michael Brown is a therapist who takes an interpersonal approach, as he is trained in psychosynthesis and adopts mandala art therapy with his clients (http://www.MichaelBrown.org. Retrieved 2 January, pp. 2–25).

Psychosynthesis uses a wide range of creative techniques and assumes that "creativity originates from different levels of the unconscious" and, by aiding creative expression, "helps people connect to different levels of their unconscious creativity" (Lombard & Müller, 2016) aiming to access their "inner guidance; their Higher Self" (Brown, http://www.MichaelBrown.org. Retrieved 2 January, pp. 2–25).

Ferrucci (1982) stated how Roberto Assagioli (1888–1974) developed psychosynthesis; described as a "comprehensive understanding of the human being" that acknowledges "the contributions of science, art and the spiritual traditions" yet adopts practical exercises such as mandala art therapy to achieve psychological and spiritual growth (p. 15).

Simmons (2001) writes how Brown suggested how working with mental imagery assists clients to create metaphors that represent the issues and conflict causing their distress. The client can then reflect on the image and engage in creative exploration, having the potential for resolution and growth.

One of Brown's clients, Diperna, described how she drew six birds in the air at the end of drawing a mandala (Glen Rogers, 2018). Brown asked her, "What is the importance of the number six?" Glen Rogers suggests "how the circle is the archetypal symbol of wholeness and unity" It turned out that when she was six years old, she had experienced trauma, which she had forgotten. The traumatic experience was then available for her to unpack, and Diperna shared, "How things are right there in front of you, and you have to acknowledge them" (Simmons, 2001, p. 16).

The indication is how mandala art therapy can enable unconscious material to emerge, which becomes available for processing.

Pluralistic Mandala Art Therapy

To work in a pluralistic therapeutic way during mandala work, the therapist will incorporate the main concepts of pluralistic therapy. Firstly, a contracting session will cover the client's expectations and possible goals for therapy. The option to work creatively would be openly discussed and the client reassured that it is their choice. If the client shows interest in working creatively then the mandala art method could be offered. I find that by reassuring the client it is their choice to work creatively begins to establish a collaborative relationship.

If the client is happy to use mandala art then the therapist will need to outline how this works and describe the potential benefits such as the symbolism in the artwork being able to access experience that is just out of awareness, which, by engaging in creative exploration, can bring insight and understanding. During this initial session, as throughout therapy, dialogical communications with purposeful (McLeod, 2018) and Socratic questions (Padesky, 1993) are essential features to encourage deep reflection by both client and therapist. For example, a purposeful question during the initial session might be, "So you said you would like to try mandala artwork; what is it that appeals to you?" The answer will be personal to the client, but in my experience, clients who have already had experience of therapy can be drawn to this novel way of working and hope it will bring new or deeper understanding in relation to their issues contributing to achieving their expectations for therapy.

In addition, assessment and feedback will be essential, and the therapist will have their particular methods of incorporating this into the therapeutic relationship. However, I believe ongoing feedback is essential in a collaborative relationship, so the client's views on how helpful the creative method is will be valuable in making any required changes to meet the client's individual needs. Therefore, regularly checking with the client to see whether any method or strategy works for them is required. Questions such as 'How did you experience that method?' and 'What did you make of it?' can encourage the client to offer their opinion and encourage autonomous thinking. If the client shares how they have achieved some insight by engaging in creative work, it might be helpful to ask, 'How do you think this realisation might help you move on?'.

The pluralistic approach appreciates methods and ways of working from various orientations. In mandala artwork, I often suggest to clients that they engage in free writing once their mandala is complete. I believe personal reflection by writing down any thoughts or feelings that come up can open up issues for processing, which had gone unaddressed previously. These reflections, along with the mandala can then be explored in the following therapy session. If the client is uncomfortable engaging with writing, they can be offered the choice of audio recording their reflections.

Mandala art therapy can be particularly useful in continuous discovery, with the client drawing subsequent mandalas on the same theme. Often, subsequent mandalas indicate progression of a particular issue, which can be very helpful in mapping the client's recovery or development.

I have worked with clients who have engaged in mandala artwork both face-to-face and in online therapy. Clients can take their time when they create their mandala between therapy sessions. I suggest they complete the mandala and do some free writing before a therapy session. This way, they can complete the mandala privately, allowing the symbols to emerge.

I also recommend that the therapist inform the client that the quality of the artwork is not important; the aim is to explore what the symbols they have drawn/painted mean to them. I usually give an example of one mandala drawn by a client with a single stick figure at the bottom of the circle, yet this symbol had a powerful meaning for the client when he felt disempowered, opening up an experience he needed to talk about and express the feelings associated with it.

With regard to online therapy, clients will either photograph their mandala or hold it up to the screen so that the therapist can see it. It can also be useful to invite the client to talk through their written reflection if they are happy to do that.

Just as with any creative strategy, a client can work in a structured or non-structured way in mandala art therapy. A structured approach may be more applicable to a client who seeks guidance from the therapist. This might occur due to the client not being familiar with creative work and needs more support from the therapist to engage.

Case Study: Jack

For example, a young male client, Jack, was preparing to go to University and live on campus. Jack's goal was for him to manage his anxiety because although he was excited about this transition, he was also struggling with nervous anxiety and finding it increasingly hard to hide from his parents. He did not want to worry his parents by talking through his anxiety with them. So, we explored the various tasks that may help him cope, such as a breathing strategy. However, Jack had tried breathing exercises before, saying they did not work. I asked him whether he was interested in working creatively, and he felt positive about trying something creative before the next session. Together, we decided to try the method of mandala ark work to see if it helped him get to the root of his anxiety. I suggested that he consider the upcoming change of leaving for university and draw his mandala, his thoughts, and feelings depicted by the symbols drawn within the circle.

In the next session, Jack shared his mandala, which showed four meer cats: standing on their hind legs, but with one turning away from the group. When Jack engaged in free writing, it appeared that part of him was feeling sad; he was anticipating leaving his mother, father and little brother. Jack had not acknowledged this upcoming loss before he reflected on his mandala, yet now began to express his sadness. We explored how any change, even a positive change, can bring loss. Over the next few sessions, he expressed and unpacked his sadness further and then focused on his preparation for the upcoming change. Giving himself permission to feel sad and still excited helped him to acknowledge that this was a 'normal' response to such a big change which brought a real sense of relief for him.

An unstructured approach involves the client engaging in mandala work without focusing on any particular issue and staying with the process to see what emerges. Working this way may be more conducive to edge-of-awareness discovery (Gendlin, 1996). The experience, out of full awareness yet accessible due to the symbolic process, helps to make the implicit explicit. The symbols drawn within the circle can also facilitate unconscious processing, with experience previously out of awareness now in consciousness for exploration (Kalff, 1980; Turner, 2005).

Case Study: Sandra's Personal Journey of Mandala Art Therapy

Sandra's presenting problem was her lack of confidence when public speaking in a formal presentation setting, which was causing her anxiety as she was on a higher education course that required such public speaking. Her goal was to try and develop her confidence in this respect. She was happy to try the method of mandala art therapy, and the following guidance was given to her:

Sandra was given several blank circles, which were pre-drawn on paper for her to use, along with the following instructions on a handout:

- Find a quiet space where you won't be disturbed.
- Have your paper and art materials to hand and focus your mind on your breathing. As you gently breathe in and out, it can help to close your eyes. Relax each part of your body in turn so that you are in a calm state before you begin to draw. Now focus on your feelings and if there is anything concerning you at this time. Begin to draw anything you want within the circle.
- "Following completion, engage in some free-writing. Write down your thoughts and feelings when observing the mandala you have drawn. Your writing does not have to be neat; the grammar has no consequence here so avoid editing your writing as you go just feel free to write down everything on the page".

Sandra's first mandala depicted the circle sectioned into two with a tiger leaping towards a retreating butterfly (Image 3.1). It appeared as if the tiger was about to attack the butterfly. Sandra shared some reflections after engaging in free writing after completing her drawing. She began by exploring what the symbols of a tiger and butterfly meant to her:

> Tiger—"symbolises strength, power and I suppose aggression".
> Butterfly—"symbolises gentleness, it is delicate, soft and can fly".

Image 3.1 Sandra's first mandala

"These two elements are in conflict. The Tiger could destroy the Butterfly. The Tiger has such power. It can protect itself and won't back off or back down. If I think of myself, I would not back down if my family were in danger. Maybe I do have part of the Tiger in me. I suppose the only other time the Tiger is apparent is when I do my martial arts. I may be small, but I can blend with another partner's energy and throw them into a break-fall, even a man who is much bigger than me.
The Butterfly is gentle and delicate—words like kind, soft, and blending come to mind. If things get too hard, it can fly away. Sometimes, in social situations, I experience shyness; part of this is that I don't feel good enough and am sensitive to criticism or being left out of the group. I am so nervous when I have to give a presentation that my whole body shakes. I know what I want to say, yet it is difficult to say it out loud and remain confident. I just cannot see how these two aspects can ever be compatible. There is no harmony between them, they are in conflict."

Purposeful questions were then asked to help Sandra deepen her reflections:

Therapist Question: 'Thinking back, what were you like as a child?'
Sandra: "When I was little Mum always said I was shy, I always sat next to her in company. She would say to the other adults, 'Oh she's just shy".
T. Question: "What do you feel now, when you hear yourself repeat your Mum's message to those adults?"
S.: "I feel a little angry….it didn't help…I feel…felt silly"
T. Question: "What would you have preferred your mum to say?"
S.: "Probably nothing, just let me be but I think I became more withdrawn"
T.: "So that message, of you being a shy child really took hold?"
S.: "Only with adults, I was confident playing with other children".
T: "But not with those you saw as more powerful than you?"
S.: "I suppose, then we had to show respect to the adults but thinking back, some of them said things, which were not nice; you know kind of judgemental of others, even then I was aware of that, but I didn't have a voice, they were grown ups". "Even now when I disagree, sometimes I will keep my view to myself. Will I ever be strong enough to face a situation when I feel judged? I find it so hard when somebody gives me that look, as if they think I am not good enough!"

My reflection to Sandra near the end of the session was, "I wonder if it would be possible to draw on the energy of the 'Tiger' and the energy of the 'Butterfly'? Both aspects appear to have something positive to offer".

Ferrucci (1982) from a psychosynthesis approach identifies aspects of Self as subpersonalities and his understanding is that creative work can help resolve inner-conflict between two elements and eventually the process of integration can occur (p. 58). With regard to Sandra, I hoped that at some point she would be able to draw on that powerful aspect of self, the tiger when preparing and delivering presentations during public speaking. In addition, the characteristics of the butterfly might also help her when a situation required gentleness. However, my intent is not to force insight but facilitate a gentle unfolding of understanding when the client is ready.

Six months later, Sandra created a second mandala and wanted to explore this in therapy. This image illustrated the same symbols but this time the butterfly was hovering over the tiger's head, as if it was attempting to land. Sandra shared:

> "I am beginning to see that both the tiger and the butterfly have something positive for me but I am still struggling to see how they can truly blend together."

I asked Sandra, could she give an example of when each aspect had helped her. She shared how she has tried to visualise the power of the tiger when beginning to speak out in a group discussion at university, which helped a little but she soon began to feel nervous, the butterfly was back, "I felt myself backing off". I attempted to encourage her by wondering whether this would take time and practice and she seemed a little more reassured and would continue to practice this strategy.

Sandra's 3rd Mandala—9 Months After Sandra Had Created Her First Mandala

Sandra had a break from therapy but nine months later, returned with a photograph of a third mandala. She shared how her confidence had grown regarding public speaking and was establishing relationships in the group setting, and shared how she was happy with her progress.

She also shared how she had been shopping and had come across an image on a t-shirt, which had a profound meaning for her. The t-shirt illustrated a beautiful Tiger's head but with Butterfly wings for ears. She shared how this image was her ideal Self for the future, which she described as the Tiger and the butterfly merging together. This powerful image encapsulated her hope for the future. For Sandra, the way she had come across this symbol was significant. For her, it represented synchronicity and validation, stating, "This is real; it is not just a feature of my imagination". There was something significant about requiring this image independently from any effort on her part—she said, "It was like this image came to me when I wasn't searching for it; it just appeared…a synchronicity!" This seemed to hold more meaning for her, giving her a sense that she was only a tiny part of a bigger picture, regarding her life. Sandra took a photograph of the image on her t-shirt, had it framed, and in her words, "It gives me hope; each one of us is only part of a much bigger tapestry".

It was apparent to me as her therapist how the concept of integration between these two originally opposing aspects was beginning to occur. Ferrucci (1982) stated, "We increase our integration by allowing our subpersonalities to become synergistic rather than antagonistic with each other" (p. 58).

Group Work

As a trainer and clinical supervisor, I have also led mandala artwork in groups. My approach here is to give some information on mandala art therapy, with examples so that the group participants can begin to appreciate its practical application. Once this theoretical introduction is complete, a handout is given with instructions to complete an individual mandala, and this is talked through, giving space for questions and answers. With participants who are not comfortable drawing or painting, I suggest that they might want to use words of varying colour to represent their experience and this has worked well for some. I remember being struck by the power of one participant writing the word 'No' in different sizes, different colours and different positions within her mandala related to historical abuse. The participant's reflections were both powerful and moving and a demonstration that a person does not have to be good at drawing to receive deep meaning from the method.

Once each participant has completed their mandala, they observe their creation and engage in some free writing. The next stage is to pair up with another person and for each to talk through their process. The advice I give the listener is to "stay with the speaker's interpretation of their symbols and not to 'step on their process' by offering your own interpretation. Be an active listener, ask questions and make reflections but keep your own interpretations to yourself".

To facilitate the group session, mandala circles that are pre-drawn on paper and art materials will be available for participants. Once each pair has talked through their process, it is helpful to have a large group feedback session. I usually inform the group that if anyone is happy to share their experience with the group they would be welcome to do so. I also facilitate feedback on how the participants experienced the session providing both verbal and written comments.

In summary, the symbols and metaphors in the client's mandala facilitate the client's engagement in creative exploration, offering potential for resolution and personal growth. Furthermore, the symbolic process can aid the client to explore 'edge of awareness' material, helping them to find their own words to describe the implicit experience. Additionally, the creative symbolism can also bring repressed unconscious material into awareness, allowing the client to process it.

The client can be invited to engage in a structured or unstructured approach. A structured approach might involve the therapist guiding them to draw a mandala of their anxiety. In comparison, an unstructured approach might involve the therapist suggesting they draw a mandala without a focus or to tune into their feelings and see what symbols emerge on the paper.

References

Babouchkina, A., & Robbins, S. J. (2015). Reducing negative mood through Mandala creation: A randomized controlled trial. *Journal of the American Art Therapy Association., 32*(1), 34–39. https://doi.org/10.1080/07421656.2015.994428

Bailey Cunningham, L. (2010). *The Mandala book*. Sterling Publishing Company.

Brown, M. H. (2001). Mandala minnow and transformations of consciousness. *3 client/artist interviews with Michael H. Brown, Ed. S.* One-hour documentary (pp. 8–13). Aired on Richmond Channel 6 TV May 25, 2001. http://www.MichaelBrown.org. Retrieved January 2025.

Fang, T. (2012). Yin Yang: A new perspective on culture. *Management and Organization Review, 8*(1), 25–50. Special Issue Indigenous Management Research in China. https://doi.org/10.1111/j.1740-8784.2011.00221.x

Ferucci, P. (1982). *What we may be: Technics for psychological and spiritual growth* (1st ed.). J. P. Tarcher, Inc.

Gendlin, E. T. (1984). The client's client: The edge of awareness. In R. L. Levant & J. M. Shlien (Eds.), *Client-centered therapy and the person-centered approach. New directions in theory, research and practice*. Praeger.

Gendlin, E. T. (1996). Focusing orientated psychotherapy. *New York: Guildford Press.*

Glen Rogers, 2018. https://artandsacredsites.com/2018/06/20/the-circle-symbol-of-wholeness/ retrieved 21 January, 2026.

Henderson, P., Rosen, D., & Mascaro, N. (2007). Empirical study of the healing nature of mandalas. *Psychology of Aesthetics, Creativity, and the Arts,* 1(13), 148-154.

Illing, H. A. (1963). Memories, dreams, reflections. *The American Journal of Psychiatry, 120*(6), 616. https://doi.org/10.1176/ajp.120.6.616

Jaeger, S. (2025). *A geomedical approach to Chinese medicine: The origin of the Yin-Yang symbol. Recent advances in theories and practice of Chinese medicine* (pp. 29–45). National Library of Medicine. United States. www.intechopen.com. Retrieved 2 January 2025.

Jung, C. G. (1964). *Civilisation in transition, collective works* (Vol. 10). Routledge and Kegan Paul.

Jung, C. G. (1972). *Mandala Symbolism.* Original publication: Vol 9, Collected Works by R.F.C. Hull. Princeton/Bollingen Paperbacks. ISBN 0-691-01781-6 90000.

Jung, C. G. (1973). *Mandala symbolism* (R. F. C. Hull, Trans.). Princeton University Press. (Original work published 1959).

Jung, C. G. (1989). *Memories, dreams, reflections.* Vintage Books.

Kalff, D. M. (1980). Sandplay. Boston: Sigo Press.

Kim, H., Kim, S., Choe, C., & Kim, J. S. (2018, April). Effects of Mandala art therapy on subjective well-being, resilience, and hope in psychiatric inpatients. *Archives of Psychiatric Nursing, 32*(2), 167–173. Elsevier Inc. Republic of Korea. https://doi.org/10.1016/j.apnu.2017.08.008. Accessed December 2024.

King, P. C., & Zhang, W. (2014). Problem solving: A test of Yin-Yang thinking. *Journal of Management and Sustainability, 4*(4), 76–85. ISSN 1925-4725 E-ISSN 1925-4733. Published by Canadian Center of Science and Education.

Kostyunina, N. Y., & Drozdikova-Zaripova, A. R. (2016). Adolescents' school anxiety correction by means of Mandala art therapy. *International Journal of Environmental & Science Education, 11*(6), 1105–1116. Kazan (Volga

region) Federal University, RUSSIA. https://doi.org/10.12973/ijese.2016.380a. LOOK Publishers.
Lombard, C. A., & Müller, B. C. (2016). Opening the door to creativity: A psychosynthesis approach. *Journal of Humanistic Psychology*. https://doi.org/10.1177/0022167816653224
McLeod, J. (2018). *Pluralistic therapy. Distinctive features*. Routledge. Taylor & Francis Group.
Padesky, C. (1993). *Socratic questioning: Changing minds or guiding discovery?* ECBT Keynote Address: London.
Pisarik, C. T., & Larson, K. R. (2011). Facilitating college students' authenticity and psychological well-being through the use of mandalas: an empirical study. *The Journal of Humanistic Counseling, 50*(1), 84–98.
Simmons, J. (2001, October). Managing Editor. Fishing for clues. *Counseling Today. American Counseling Association Publication*, 14–16.
Turner, B. A. (2005). *The handbook of Sandplay therapy*. Temenos Press.
Xinyan, X. (2013). Chinese dialectical thinking—The Yin Yang model. *Philosophy Compass, 8*(5), 76–85. https://doi.org/10.1111/phc3.12035

4

Writing in Therapy

Writing can be a powerful tool for self-expression. Ullrich and Lutgendorf (2002) suggested how "writing about stressors or traumatic events has been associated with improvements in mental health in numerous investigations" (p. 244). Other researchers argue how this writing strategy contributes to a decrease in distress (Donnelly & Murray, 1991), improvements in psychological well-being and physical health (Smyth, 1998). Moreover, a systematic review of 31 studies by Porras-Segovia et al. (2024) showed how creative writing significantly improved depression (p. 359). Conversely, inhibition of emotion is considered harmful (Rachman, 1980), and Ullrich and Lutgendorf (2002) described this as a chronic stressor that can lead to decreased emotional and physical health.

Gratz and Roemer (2004) suggest emotional regulation is the ability to understand and control impulsive actions when distressed and modify emotional expression appropriate to the context. Furthermore, Sargunarai et al. (2021) argued that therapeutic writing was a helpful strategy for achieving emotional regulation. Similarly, Wisco et al. (2013) argued how "cognitive emotion regulation and written exposure therapy for post-traumatic stress disorder decreased non-suicidal self-injury and decreased post-traumatic disorder symptoms" (p. 435).

D. Fleet, *Creative Interventions in Counselling and Psychotherapy*, Palgrave Texts in Counselling and Psychotherapy, https://doi.org/10.1007/978-3-032-16609-8_4

In my experience with clients who struggle to express emotion related to distressing experience, a current painful experience can trigger emotions from previous disturbing events; the client can then become overwhelmed as the repressed emotion resurfaces. An example of this is how a current bereavement can trigger an unresolved loss, exacerbating the individual's emotional distress.

Hunt and Sampson (1998) describe how Virginia Woolf wrote about the impact of her mother dying when Woolf was only 13 years old. In 1989, Woolf began writing down her long-felt deep emotions, enabling her to express, understand, and lay those emotions to rest (DeSalvo, 1989, p. 90). She likened this to the process of psychoanalysis by getting to the root cause of her pain regarding the death of her mother.

Munson (2000) in line with Woolf's perspective on the power of writing, stated, "writing splints the wounded body" enabling recovery, to rest, enabling "reconstruction to occur" (p. 24). Pennebaker and Chung (1984) suggested how writing in therapy decreased stress in an individual experiencing post-traumatic stress disorder (PTSD). Furthermore, Pizarro (2004) argues how expressive writing such as journaling helped individuals deal with complex emotions by developing their capabilities, bringing healing, and change. Furthermore, expressive writing can contribute to positive physical and psychological outcomes in those who have experienced traumatic bereavement (Frattaroli, 2006).

Many of my clients who engage in journal writing between sessions, have experienced a shift in their thinking and emotional state relating to new understanding of their issues.

Case Study: Joan

Joan, whose mother suddenly died was trying to cope with her grief, yet the death of her grandmother many years ago, when Joan was a child, was also occupying her mind and emotional state, which was confusing to her.

Joan was happy to work on her journaling in between therapy sessions and bring her reflections to the sessions so I could help her in deeper exploration.

Joan began by writing down her thoughts and feelings concerning both losses, beginning with the death of her beloved grandmother. She was only 9 years old when her grandmother died, Joan did not attend the funeral, and there was an avoidance to talk about her grandmother's death in the family. Joan shared,

> "I think they didn't want me to be sad. I loved her, but she was gone, I didn't get to say goodbye...it's like that loss has come up from nowhere".

In the therapy session, we also discussed how an unresolved loss from the past could be triggered by a current loss and this had the effect of normalising Joan's experience relating to her unresolved grief. She began to realise she had not grieved the death of her grandmother, and she was then able to permit herself to grieve both losses.

Participating in writing between therapy sessions has an additional benefit. Joan's reflections and insights were explored collaboratively and offering validation to her reflections helped her develop self-acceptance as she shared her story. Furthermore, Sargunarai et al. (2021) suggested how writing in therapy related to emotional expression is potentially beneficial with the client learning how to accept and express their emotions in a manner where they do not feel overwhelmed and out of control.

Sloan and Marx (2008) suggested how expressive writing "allows an individual to be exposed to aversive stimuli that have previously been avoided" (p. 124). In Joan's case, the grief process appeared to have been disrupted by her family's good intentions of wanting to protect her from experiencing loss and pain. However, it became apparent that this impeded Joan from the opportunity to grieve her grandmother when she was 9 years old, yet now, as an adult; her psyche was giving her that opportunity to grieve.

When working with the client to explore their expressive writing, the pluralistic therapist will ask Socratic (Padesky, 1993) and purposeful questions about the client's reflections to facilitate 'metacommunication' (McLeod, 2018), aiding deeper reflection. Often, the client can expand their understanding by taking part in such mutual dialogue. Furthermore, sharing their discovery with the therapist can help the client feel heard and validated.

Hunt (2000) describes how she began to engage in writing on images that arose in therapy and then explored them in subsequent therapy sessions that helped her find her personal truth about herself (p. 10).

Free Writing

In my online practice, I regularly offer the writing strategy with clients who want to work creatively in that way. Some engage in free writing that accesses their intra-psychic experience including 'edge of awareness' discovery (Gendlin, 1984) and unconscious processing of issues relating to their concerns and distress. Free writing allows the words to be written without reflection or correcting grammar, enabling a process more "spontaneous and more directly related to the writer's inner life" (Hunt, 2000, p. 172).

This way of writing prevents any conscious reasoning, with the writer not editing or changing the content; once the person becomes familiar with this type of writing, it can feel as if the words just flow onto the page, with time passing very quickly. Hunt (2000) suggests how this "free, uncrafted writing…may be a way of getting in touch with the real material of the self" (p. 174).

I have often heard clients say things like, 'The words just appeared on the page; it was my hand that wrote, but without me thinking, it seemed to come from a deeper part in me'; and 'It was such a moving experience like my brain wasn't involved at all'. Reflection occurs when the client begins to read over and consider what they have written, as well as sharing in therapy.

Journaling

Some clients request guidance on what to focus on when journaling, so a structured approach may be more appropriate. Sargunarai et al. (2021) suggested how structured daily writing tasks with probes and questions was effective for establishing emotional regulation.

For example, some of my clients described how they find it difficult to express their anger, perceiving it as wrong or too frightened they may lose control. I have found it helpful to suggest that they begin to express their anger in their journal and guide them by asking the Socratic question:

> "If your anger had a voice, what might it say?"

This way of expressing their anger seems to permit them to begin to 'own' their anger and change their view that expressing anger is wrong. The rescripting of the message they received, often in childhood can free them into expressing anger in a safe and acceptable manner. When clients realise that righteous anger needs expressing, and they express this in a way that is not detrimental to them or others, it can bring much relief.

Ullrich and Lutgendorf (2002) suggest that journal writing that focuses on cognitions and emotions contributes to improved mental health.

When working with clients who use journaling in between sessions, I suggest that they write about their story, involving their thoughts and feelings regarding their stressful or traumatic experience. The aim here is to begin to unpack their thoughts as well as express their emotions, providing the opportunity to gain understanding and relief from emotional expression. Pennebaker and Beall (1986) argued how writing about the facts of a traumatic event as well as feelings resulted in greater improvements in mental health.

Furthermore, talking through their journal entries in therapy provides a safe environment and enables further emotional expression and insight, helped by the therapist's responses to the client's communication. Scheff (1979) appears to support this stance suggesting how a safe environment for an individual to express trauma-related experience fosters feelings of control and proficiency over the traumatic event.

The therapist offering acceptance and validation contributes to the client feeling "that their subjective experience is both respected and progressively understood" (Carl Rogers in Thorne & Sanders, 1992, p. 26).

Adopting a Creative Approach in Journaling

Capacchione suggests how journal writing can be "done through different forms of expression" (1979, p. 6) and many clients find the use of drawing, symbols, photographs, images, and colour helpful in expressing their thoughts and feelings. Rosen and Atkins (2014) stated "that using drawing tools" (i.e. crayons, colour and charcoal pencils etc.) without trying to create something specific, when followed by journaling, seems to reach beyond psychological and emotional defences" (p. 293).

Case Study—Craig

Craig pasted an image of a three-headed dog into his journal (Image 4.1). This represented the anger expressed towards him as a child from a parent. Craig was never physically hit, but the verbal abuse he received from his parents, he found extremely threatening.

Image 4.1 Three-headed dog

Craig was able to tell his story in his journal and began to express the fear he felt as a child. He reflected on the severity of his parent's reaction regarding commonplace childish behaviour. As an adult, Craig also began to realise that the label he was given as a young boy by his parents of "naughty child" was incorrect. In his words,

> "They were the ones who were wrong…with them, I could never do anything right".

This realisation helped Craig to offer self-compassion and come to the conclusion that if his parents had been supportive, patient, and gentle with him as a child, his childhood could have been very different. Furthermore, the message he received and internalised that he was 'bad' began to fade, bringing much relief for Craig.

Creativity can help clients explore freely, opening up a process that can bring fresh insight and allow them to adopt a process of expansive discovery in addition to emotional expression.

The following purposeful questions can be used as a prompt for the therapist, which may help with the client's journal reflections during a therapy session:

- What memories come up for you now when you read your writing?
- What stands out to you about this journal entry?
- What feelings did you experience when you were writing?
- What are your feelings now as you reflect on what you wrote?
  - If that feeling had a voice, what might it say?
- (If the client has written about another person who hurt them in some way):
  - If this person were sitting here in front of you, what would you need to say to them?
  - (If that person had hurt them when the client was a child) What would your 7 year old (e.g. age) say to them now?
- Is there anything you need to change, going forward?
- Do you have a goal moving forward?

Letters in Therapy

Unsent Letter

A therapist can suggest to a client how writing an unsent letter can be a helpful way of expressing unresolved issues with another person who has hurt them in the past. Adams (1990) suggested how writing an unsent letter to another person could be a helpful strategy in therapy, with such letters having a cathartic impact. Unexpressed intense emotions related to the abuse suffered such as hurt, fear, shame, rage, and betrayal could be expressed in a safe context. Writing a letter can externalise such feelings and enable the client to 'take one step out' of their overwhelming emotion, enabling them to express the lingering pain they may have repressed for some time.

Often, with issues such as abuse, abandonment, or being bullied, the client does not experience closure, which can add to their lingering pain, as it may be impossible to confront the perpetrator. For example, the client may fear confrontation, or they may now have a more positive relationship with them and not want to jeopardise that. Furthermore, the perpetrator may not take any accountability for the harm they caused or may blame the client for what happened. Moreover, the perpetrator may say, 'That happened so long ago; why are you bringing this up now, just forget it and move on?' which can minimise the harm done to the client. At other times, the perpetrator may have died or moved to another location in another part of the world. Even if a perpetrator apologises, the client may not be given space to unpack the pain inflicted.

One way of taking a step towards closure is if the therapist suggests to the client that they write an unsent letter to the person who hurt them and once written to either cut it up or burn it. This ritual of cutting up or burning can bring some relief for the client, 'taking one step towards closure'.

Depending on the intensity of unresolved emotion and intrusive thoughts, the client may find that repeating this unsent letter strategy helpful.

In my practice with clients who engage in unsent letter writing in between therapy sessions, I find that clients sharing their letter in sessions to be extremely effective. Their own voice is acknowledged both by themselves and the therapist. Often, with deeper reflection the client moves to a state where they voice, 'I no longer allow X to have power over me' and now the symbolic process of letting go can begin.

Letters to Self

Letter from a Future Self

Writing letters to Self can be an effective way of expressing intense emotions and an easier way of sharing experiences in therapy. Voskanova (2015) suggested how a client writing a letter expressing their shame is "easier for individuals to write rather than speak" (p. 56). Kress et al. (2008) suggested how writing a letter to Self when a client has experienced sexual abuse could help externalise the experience. For example, the letter may be from their future, allowing them to move beyond their present state, feeling less overwhelmed and more empowered, giving hope and the possibility of recovery.

Compassionate Letter to Self

Writing a compassionate letter to Self can also help clients who tend to self-blame. Some clients might find it hard when their tendency to blame themselves for past difficulties is severe. It can help the client to imagine receiving a letter from someone who cares for them and wants to support them in this difficult time. The aim here is to help the client begin to move from self-blame to self-compassion.

Imagine Writing a Letter to a Dear Friend/Young Sibling Who Is Struggling with the Same Issue as You

Often, when a client has been abused or abandoned, self-blame is common, and it can be difficult for them to offer self-compassion. The therapist can suggest to clients that if a dear friend or younger sibling they cared for were going through a similar issue, what would they write to help them through this difficult time? This reminds the client of their inner survival resources. Then, visualising themselves offering support and compassion to another, with the therapist's input, can help them see that they can also benefit from self-compassion, helping them move away from a self-punishing position.

Writing a Letter to a Part of Self

In my work with adult clients who have experienced insufficient love, care and compassion from caregivers, the unsent letter to their Inner Child continues to be highly effective. The client may have been abused, neglected, abandoned, or mistreated in some way during childhood by adults who were in a position of care.

Whitfield (1987) suggests how a child growing up in a dysfunctional family will experience an interruption of their "healthy neurological and psychological growth and development of the child from birth to adulthood" (p. xvi). Then, to survive, the child's Real Self (Inner Child) "goes into hiding, deep within the unconscious" (p. xvi). To recover from such suffering, the adult needs to accurately name the painful childhood experiences (Whitfield, 1987) to gain insight regarding the impact of their childhood, learn to tolerate emotional pain and find meaning in life.

It can help the client connect with their inner child if they imagine a specific age as a child not receiving the care they should have. In addition, they may have had a shortened name (*nickname*) to address the letter to so that they could connect to their thoughts and feelings at that age. It can also help some clients if they have a photograph of themselves at that age so they can observe themselves back then when writing the letter. Some clients who do not have a photograph may want to draw themselves as a child.

In addition, it can help to give some guidance on how to begin the letter, such as:

> Hi '*their nickname*' what do you want to tell me?

and then continue writing in a conversational style. I always prepare the client by saying, 'It is likely that this exercise will bring up powerful emotions for you as you connect with your younger self, so self-care is important when you engage with this exercise. A two-way discussion then takes place concerning the support they have and how they can take care of themselves during and after they finish writing the letter. Some clients might want to read the letter to a relative or friend they know will be supportive, while others will lock away their letter so that no one else can read it.

Letter to a Loved One Who Has Died

When someone has been bereaved and is struggling with the grief process, it can help if they write a letter to the deceased. Writing allows them to say the things they did not say, apologise for something they regret, and share their thoughts and feelings concerning the behaviour of the deceased when alive if there are unresolved feelings that need to be expressed. Additionally, it might be that the bereft want to share how much they miss that person.

Therapist to Client

Some therapists find that sending therapeutic letters to clients has much value both to the client and in establishing a good therapeutic relationship. Pyle (2006) suggested "many practitioners have explored and described the use of therapeutic letters" (p. 18) and how some clients "enjoyed the personal nature of the letters they received" (p. 28). Therapeutic letters sent to clients "with therapeutic intentions not only summarise the content of a session and perhaps note a future appointment, but also contribute to the therapeutic process" (Pyle, 2006, p. 18).

I often write therapy letters to my online clients part way through the counselling process. My approach is to adopt a positive, caring, and compassionate attitude when writing the letter. I have included a draft letter (below), which demonstrates my approach. However, my advice would be that you design the letter in a personal manner for each individual client.

Dear X,
First, I am grateful for the opportunity to work with you to help you work on your (the client's issues) causing you distress. So far, in our work together, you have demonstrated openness and commitment in your weekly counselling sessions.
It comes across how your past is a significant factor in your present difficulties, but I see how you have embraced the process by sharing your experiences. I also appreciate how you have talked through your reflections in your journal between sessions, which helps me stay in the loop regarding your process.
Since we began working together, I believe your progress has been developing well, which gives me hope that you will continue to heal and achieve the expectations you communicated in that first session we had together.
I also want to say that I hope you will begin to see what I and others see in you—that you are good enough and that sometimes it is OK not to excel in everything you do.
Your willingness to share your vulnerabilities and strengths makes our work feel authentic.
I look forward to continue to work with you until the time when ending feels right for you.
Best wishes,
Doreen

A Word of Caution

When deciding to use therapy letters with clients, I would advise the therapist to ask the client whether they would like to receive such letters. One consideration is that a client who is in an abusive relationship might not have the privacy of receiving letters (either by post or email) that other clients might. For example, an abusive partner may get access to the letter, which might exacerbate the client's life, putting them at risk. At other times, a client might be the only person aware they are having therapy, so receiving a letter might compromise their anonymity.

Poetry

Wilson (2010) argued "poetry is an excellent tool for the psychotherapist" (p. 1). When attempting to write a poem for therapy, the therapist would need to reassure the client that the meaning is the most important factor and that the client should not focus on grammar but write in a free-flowing way.

Wilson (2010) goes on to suggest how "poetic expression provides innermost thoughts, transcends the superficial and in many cases demonstrates the arousal of emotions" (p. 1) and often provides access to unconscious thinking.

In my practice, when a client writes a poem and wants to explore it in a therapy session, sometimes the client will want to read it out loud or give it to me to read before exploring it further.

Such creative work can help a client communicate complicated issues and distressing emotions effectively. Exploring the poem in a session can validate the client, and positive feedback, including acknowledgement, encouragement, and recognition from the therapist, can contribute to the client's self-esteem.

In summary, writing in therapy can be an effective strategy, aiding the therapeutic process. Personal expression of thoughts, feelings, and sometimes unconscious communication that has not been explored in previous sessions can alert the therapist to help the client engage in deeper exploration.

However, the choice of engaging in journal writing, poetry or writing letters needs to be the client's decision and a collaborative discussion between the client and the therapist can facilitate this.

References

Adams, K. (1990). *Journal to the Self: Twenty-two paths to personal growth. Open the door to self-understanding – by writing, reading, and creating a journal of your life.* Warner Book, Inc. ISBN: 978-0-7595-2511-5

Capacchione, L. (1979). *The creative journal.* The art of finding yourself. Newcastle Publishing Co., Inc.
DeSalvo, L. (1989). *Virginia Woolf: the impact of Childhood Sexual Abuse on her life and work.* Beacon Pr. 0807063266
Donnelly, D. A., & Murray, E. J. (1991). Cognitive and emotionl changes in written essays and therapy interventions. *Journal of Social & Clinical Psychology, 10*, 334–350.
Frattaroli, J. (2006). Experimental disclosure and its moderators: A meta-analysis. *Psychological Bulletin, 132*(6), 823–865. https://doi.org/10.1037/0033-2909.132.6.823
Gendlin, E. T. (1984). *The client's client: The edge of awareness.* In R. L. Levant & J. M. Shlien (Eds.), *Client-centered therapy and the person-centered approach. New directions in theory, research and practice*. Praeger.
Gratz, K. L., & Roemer, L. (2004). Multidimensional assessment of emotion regulation and dysregulation: development, factor structure, and initial validation of the difficulties in emotion regulation scale. *Journal of Psychopathology Behaviour Assessment, 26*(1), 41–544.
Hunt, C. (2000). *Therapeutic dimensions of autobiography in creative writing.* Jessica Kingsley Publishers Ltd.
Hunt, C., & Sampson, F. (1998). *The self on the page. Theory and practice of creative writing in personal development.* Jessica Kingsley Publishers.
Kress, V. E., Hoffman, R., & Thomas, A. M. (2008). Letters from the future: The use of therapeutic letter writing in counseling sexual abuse survivors. *Journal of Creativity in Mental Health, 3*(2), 105–118. https://doi.org/10.1080/15401380802226497
McLeod, J. (2018). *Pluralistic therapy. Distinctive features*. Routledge. Taylor & Francis Group.
Munson, P. (2000). Criminal language and poetic jailbreak: Writing chronic fatigue immune dysfunction syndrome. *Literature and Medicine, 19*(1), 19–24.
Padesky, C. (1993). *Socratic Questioning: Changing minds or guiding discovery?* ECBT Keynote Address: London.
Pennebaker, J. W., & Beall, S. K. (1986). Confronting a traumatic event: Towad an understanding of inhibition and disease. *Journal of Abnormal Psychology, 95*, 247–281.
Pennebaker, J. W., & Chung, C. K. (1984). Expressive writing: Connections to physical and mental Health. In H. S. Friedman (Ed.), *Oxford handbook of health psychology* (pp. 417–437). Oxford Library of Psychology.

Pizarro, J. (2004). The efficacy of art and writing therapy: Increasing positive mental health outcomes and participant retention after exposure to traumatic experience. *Art Therapy, 21*(1), 5–12.

Porras-Segovia, A., Escobedo-Aedo, P. J., Carrillo de Albornoz, C. M., Guerrero-Jim.nez, M., Lis, L., Molina-Madue, R., Gutiérrez-Rojas, L., & Alacreu, A. (2024). Writing to keep on living: A systematic review and meta-analysison creative writing therapy for the management of depression and suicidal ideation. *Current Psychiatry Reports, 26*, 359–378. https://doi.org/10.1007/s11920-024-01511-6

Pyle, N. R. (2006). Therapeutic Letters in Counselling Practice: Client and Counsellor Experiences. *Canadian Journal of Counselling*, 40(1), 17–31.

Rachman, S. J. (1980). Emotional processing. *Behaviour Research in Therapy, 18*, 51–60.

Rosen, C. M., & Atkins, S. S. (2014). Perspectives. Am I doing expressive arts therapy or creativity in counseling? *Journal of Creativity in Mental Health, 9*, 292–303. https://doi.org/10.1080/15401383.2014.906874

Sargunarai, M., Kashyap, H., & Chandra, P. S. (2021). Writing your way through feelings: Therapeutic writing for emotion regulation. *Journal of Psychosocial Rehabilitation, Mental Health, 8*, 73–79. https://doi.org/10.1007/s40737-020-00198-1

Scheff, T. T. (1979). *Catharsis in healing, ritual and drama.* University of California Press.

Sloan, D. & Marx, B. P. Epstein, E. M. & Dobbs, L. (2008). Expressive writing buffers against maladaptive rumination. Emotion, Vol 8(2), Apr 2008, 302-306

Smyth, J. M. (1998). Written emotional expression. Effect sizes, outcomes types and moderating variables. *Journal of Consulting and Clinical Psychology, 66*, 174–184.

Thorne, B., & Sanders, P. (1992). *Carl Rogers.* Sage Publications Ltd. ISBN 9781446291177.

Ullrich, P., & Lutgendorf, S. K. (2002). Journaling about stressful events: Effect of cognitive processing and emotional expression. *The Society of Behavioral Medicine, 24*(3), 244–250.

Voskanova, C. (2015). A letter does not blush: In-session writing to deal with shame in brief therapy. *Journal of Family Psychotherapy, 26*(1), 56–61. https://doi.org/10.1080/08975353.2015.1002744

Whitfield, C. L. (1987). *Healing the child within: Discovery and recovery for adult children of dysfunctional families.* Health Communications Inc.

Wilson, B. (2010). Using poetry in psychotherapy. *International Journal of Scholarly Academic Intellectual Diversity, 12*(1), 1–20.

Wisco, B. E., Sloan, D. M., & Marx, B. P. (2013). Cognitive emotion regulation and written exposure therapy for posttraumatic stress disorder. *Clinical Psychology Science, 1*(4), 435–442. https://doi.org/10.1177/2167702613486630

5
Working with Music

Since ancient times, music has been used to enhance well-being and reduce suffering (Kemper and Danhauer (2005). Kemper and Danhauer (2005) argued how listening to music can have a direct physiological effect on a person's autonomic nervous system that contributes to reducing anxiety.

Furthermore, several research studies argue how interventions using music facilitate changes in emotion (Holland, 1995; Scott, 2007/2008; Smeijsters, 1995). Such changes in emotion can help clients who experience sadness, hopelessness, and mood disorders, such as depression and psychological changes (Punkanen et al., 2011).

Moreover, Illie and Thompson (2011) highlight how music connects with the body as well as psychological and emotional states. Hargreaves et al. (2012) argued that music is a type of communication that significantly changes difficult emotions. I reiterate this argument and have observed such shifts with clients. From a personal perspective, if I am nervous or worried about an upcoming experience, I often listen to a piece of music that is either relaxing or motivating, and I usually sense a real movement in my attitude.

D. Fleet, *Creative Interventions in Counselling and Psychotherapy*, Palgrave Texts in Counselling and Psychotherapy, https://doi.org/10.1007/978-3-032-16609-8_5

Leijssen (2006) argued how verbal psychotherapy can be improved by "adding a bodily perspective" (p. 126). Although most therapeutic approaches incorporate the client's nonverbal cues, this is dissimilar to adopting body-orientated interventions that focus on the client on what is sensed inside their body (Leijssen, 2006).

Focusing on inner bodily experience can often help the client develop "greater awareness, engagement in the present…cathartic release (Leijssen, 2006, p. 126) and helps to resolve blocks.

When a client is listening to a piece of music in a therapy session, once the music stops, I will ask, 'What feelings came up for you when you were listening?' The client might say, 'Sad…I feel sad. Then, when I ask where they feel the sadness in their body, once they respond, I will guide them to place their hands on that part of the body, followed by the question, 'If that sadness had a voice, what would it say?' My understanding is that listening to their inner thoughts, feelings, and bodily sensations in response to the music can deepen reflection, facilitating insight and bring up unexpressed emotions, which can then be processed.

Armstrong (2015) also argued that music impacts the brain, calms anxiety, and facilitates insight for the individual. Furthermore, from a neuroscience standpoint, Armstrong suggests how music "stimulates the reward and pleasure centres of the brain by releasing endogenous opioids, even if the music is sad" (Armstrong, 2015, p. 140). Kawakami et al. (2013) supported this stance, arguing how listening to sad music can produce positive emotions. Huron and Marguilis (2010) describe how emotive music that brings "thrills or chills' activates the pleasure centres in the brain".

Armstrong (2015) goes on to argue that listening to melancholy music does not necessarily result in worsening feelings of sadness and depression due to "vicarious rather than direct emotion" (p. 141). I would add, a client listening to such melancholy music helps them take one step out of their pain but without losing connection to it. This type of externalisation can help the person express their sadness without becoming overwhelmed.

Working with Music in a Group Setting

Music can be a helpful topic when delivering a workshop to a student group, a group of therapist supervisees or clients in group therapy.

Case Study: Workshop on Using Music with a Group of Psychotherapy Students

I delivered a workshop on using music for a group of students on a psychotherapy course to help with their personal development and to consider the possibility of using music in therapy. However, this workshop could be adapted for a client group or a clinical supervision group.

Prior to the workshop, my first task was to prepare a recording of different sections of music. Each piece of music had differences in tempo, pitch, harmony, melody, rhythm, pace, tone and style to factor in variation. The twelve pieces of music selected were instrumental without speech and each lasted approximately one minute, with a few seconds gap between each. I also provided paper and pens.

The group in this example was diverse as there was variation in sex, gender, age, ethnicity and social background. Each person was given a piece of paper and pen along with the following instructions that were also verbally communicated by myself as facilitator:

- Listen to each piece of music that will last one minute and write down single words of your thoughts and feelings for each piece. This might be one word or more.
- On completion, reflect on the list of words you have produced and create a piece of writing or poem, using your words. You will have 30 minutes to complete this and I will inform you when you have 5 minutes left. Please remember the most important thing is the personal meaning your writing has for you. This exercise is about helping you and not impressing anyone else.
- This exercise works best when the room is quiet so please avoid talking when the music is playing and when you are engaged in writing your piece.

- Once the 30 minutes is up, please come back to the group so we can have a group debrief. Here you have the opportunity to share your writing/poem with the rest of the group if you are happy to do so and listen to others who are willing to share theirs.
- The final section will focus on your experience of engaging in this exercise.

Lasting impressions of me as the facilitator of this group:

The Ubiquitous Nature of Music.

Despite differences in age, gender and background, all individuals responded to each piece of music played, expressing their thoughts and feelings. This gave me the confidence that the majority of people would likely engage with the activity in their own way but also to have a good range of different pieces of music so as to suit different preferences.

Impact of the Music Played in the Workshop:

- Evoked memories for some individuals.
- Evoked powerful feelings (love, tenderness, connection, joy, loss, sadness, anger, resentment, hurt).
- Connections to others (relationships positive and negative/happy and painful).
- Connecting to aspects of Self (Inner-life—Inner-Child, Determined Self, Hurt Part of Self, Abandoned Self).
- Insight—fresh perspectives (need for bringing change).
- Connecting to a worldly perspective (moving from the individual to the universal, sense of connectedness, spiritual connection, care for others across the globe).
- Spiritual focus (desire for continued spiritual growth).

In the feedback section of the workshop, all individuals enjoyed the activity despite some being a little nervous to begin with. They had shared personal experiences and were respectful by listening and valuing when others shared theirs. As the facilitator, I found the session both moving and enlightening. About half of the attendees created a poem, while others produced a piece of writing that was moving, insightful and perceptive.

As a facilitator, I asked the question about the writing task. Some members of the group felt the guidance on simply writing a piece was welcome, they shared that to have only said they write a poem would have been too intimidating for some, perceiving this as a skill they did not have.

Before the session, I wondered whether some of the group might not have received the workshop well, however I was pleasantly surprised by how each participant engaged with the whole process. One piece of feedback from the participants was that they would have liked me, as a facilitator, to have produced a piece of writing to share. One individual said, 'We are sharing personal stuff here, so it would have been good for you to have shared something personal'. I thanked the group for this feedback and said I would definitely consider doing that in my next music workshop.

My dilemma was that although I wanted to take this feedback on board, I also needed to support anyone who needed help with the exercise as powerful emotions might have surfaced for some. However, it was an interesting offer, which I considered for the next workshop I delivered.

On reflection, my decision was to prepare a personal piece prior to the group activity then ask the group if they wanted to hear my own writing once they had shared theirs.

Clients Selecting Music to Play in Therapy Sessions

Särkämö et al. (2008) explored how stroke patients who selected pieces of music to listen to indicated a significant reduction in their depression and confused states. Furthermore, MacDonald (2013) suggested that a client's preference is key when choosing music as it facilitates the therapeutic process. Taverne and Nicholls (2025) argued how accepting the music the client brings, is appreciating their language, you as therapist communicate that they matter which helps to build a deeper connection. Furthermore, facilitating a client to select a piece of music to play in a therapy session recognises the client as an active participant (Fairchild, 2018) in the relationship, which is compatible with the pluralistic approach that values collaboration between therapist and client.

Case Study—Liz Selecting a Piece of Music to Play in a Therapy Session

During the initial session, Liz shared how she had a tendency to avoid her feelings. When she was a child, her father was sent to prison and incarcerated for several years. Her mother had the attitude of 'we need to be strong and get on with things', which resulted in Liz internalizing this message and not expressing her loss. This behaviour of staying positive and getting on with things had a lasting impact on Liz, as avoiding powerful feelings as an adult became part of who she was. Her tendency was to make jokes, laugh and berate herself when she began to feel moments of sadness or fear.

Liz's goal for therapy was to stay with and express her feelings, and she set me the task of helping her to do that. In order to establish the method for me to help her meet this goal, we engaged in a two-way conversation. We decided that I would challenge her when I observed her moving away from her feelings by making comments like, 'You seem to be avoiding your loss here, or I notice it is hard for you to stay with your sadness.'

Even though we had agreed on the method of Liz staying with her feelings, she soon began to engage in her pattern of avoidance.

In one session, Liz was focusing on the time her father was taken away, and she struggled to stay with this tremendous loss, and any attempt by me to help her express her pain failed.

Near the end of the session, we had a collaborative discussion, and I shared how I was finding it challenging to help her stay with her painful feelings. Liz then shared, "I know, I always manage to slip away from going there". She then shared how "the only thing that works for me is music; some tracks bring tears to my eyes". Liz's comment was a 'green light' for me, and I responded, 'that strategy might help you in the session. What do you think about bringing in a piece of music to play in the following session that might help you stay with your feelings?' Liz was happy to do this, and in the next session, we had a breakthrough; when listening to the music, she began to express her sadness concerning the loss and her fear of her Dad being taken away. Liz began to regularly listen to music at home that evoked painful feelings without avoidance. In the past she would have left the room or turned off the music but she continued to build her commitment to express her pain.

In pluralistic therapy, it is important for the therapist to listen to the client when they signal a way of working. This collaborative relationship not only helps the therapeutic process but also facilitates client autonomy, with them contributing to the process. It is also an opportunity for the therapist to offer acknowledgement and validation by facilitating a purposeful dual discussion when considering a new method by asking questions to help the client engage in reflection.

Case Study—Julia a Carer for Her Disabled Mother

Julia was a carer for her disabled mother. Julia described how she had to stay strong as her Mother was moving towards the end of life and was fearful of dying. Julia kept her Mother home as long as she could before being moved to a hospice. Julia was that last relative of her immediate family so the responsibility of caring for her mother and once her mother had died, organizing the funeral.

After several months of caring for her mother, Julia had a strong coping attitude and if tears came she would stop them. "Seems like for months and months I kept myself busy, crying wouldn't have helped me or my Mum". Six months after her mother had died, Julia attended the musical 'Les Miserables' and shared how her tears began to flow during the song of "I dreamed a dream', stating, "it was nothing to do with the story...it was all about my Mum".

Mount (2018) argued how the client and therapist listening to a song (or piece of music) chosen by the client can facilitate discussion of the client's feelings and personal history and help to process powerful emotions.

Julia and I decided to listen to this song together in a session. Julia's eyes filled up with tears, and the music somehow got through the block Julia had created as a way of coping. I also had tears in my eyes as we listened to this song together, which brought a sense of connectedness between us.

After we discussed our experience, Julia shared how good it felt to let her sadness out by crying. We then explored her sadness and pain, not only the loss of her mother but the lingering way her Mother's health declined and how Julia felt this was so unfair. "She was such a loving woman, she didn't deserve that".

Case Study Liam—Expressing Anger

Liam had overly strict and dominant parents. He shared,

> "When I was a child they were mean for the sake of it, always criticizing, even now as an adult they just don't seem to care about me. As a kid all I heard was QUIET, QUIET, QUIET!!" "Can't remember any time they were kind to me, like I couldn't be me, couldn't breathe, always being told I was naughty".
> I feel an ache in here (touched his chest) when I think of them and how they treated me. I can't bring myself to even visit them now they are old. I've been angry for so long. Went off the rails for a while as a teenager, not that they cared. Now I feel my anger differently. My music is a way I can let it out. The track Thunder Struck by AC/DC is a good one for me".

I responded by asking, so does that track help you express your anger? Liam replied, "yeah…I can play it if you want". I responded, "what a good idea".

Liam used his IPhone to play 'Thunderstuck' by AC/DC and we listened to this together. Once the track had finished, I asked Liam how he felt?

> "It's like my anger is speaking. Screaming 'thunder' – letting it out, feels good, I do that when I am alone".

Liam had shared a raw and personal aspect of himself and I felt privileged that he did that. I replied by saying, "I am so glad that you could share that with me, such a powerful track".

He responded, "you listened"

I responded to him by saying, 'felt quite cathartic, you know, like giving your anger a voice'.

He replied, "That's just it – you get it".

Listening to Liam's choice of music felt good, as well as offering him understanding and empathy I also felt included in his process. By validating his choice of music and communicating the benefit of this strategy helped us make a connection. This gave him the experience of creatively expressing his anger in a safe way.

Therapeutic Songwriting

Baker and Ballantyne (2012) suggested therapeutic songwriting was another method of using music in therapy that was a way of exploring Self and enhancing mood. In the counselling setting it might be more applicable for the client to engage in such musical songwriting outside of the therapeutic session and then to write a journal entry on how they felt during and after the task, which can then be explored in the subsequent therapy session.

Case Study—Charles and Therapeutic Songwriting

In his initial session, Charles presented with depression and having no work-life balance. It came to pass that he used to play the guitar, and I helped him explore how he felt when he played. He became more animated, expressing his passion, as he recalled his past activity with music and how he loved to write songs. "Time just flew, I used to really enjoy myself".

This experience of losing time is supported by MacDonald (2013), who suggests how individuals lose track of time and experience a feeling of flow when engaged in songwriting. I asked Charles, "How would it be if each day he found some time to go back to playing his guitar?" After some discussion, we established a goal for him to play his guitar for 30 minutes each evening before his evening meal. The following week, he shared how, although he was somewhat ‘rusty’, he had been able to play for three days and enjoyed it. We also discussed the impact on Charles when and after playing his guitar. He shared how it helped him forget his worries, he felt less stressed, far more relaxed in a physical way and his wife liked listening to it too. Byrne (2012) stated, “Music tells us things – social things, psychological things, physical things about how we feel and perceive our bodies – in a way that other art forms can’t” (p. 101).

After 3 weeks of regularly playing his guitar, Charles began to see this as self-care and not just a task. In the fourth week, he began to ponder writing his own songs, and we decided to incorporate this activity into his music routine each evening. A month later, he shared how he was totally absorbed in songwriting and decided he would write a song for his wife’s birthday and sing it to her. In the following session, Charles was happy to share how much she loved it. He found this validation encouraging, and he decided to continue with his music playing as it was positively impacting his mood.

Gilsum (Bruscia & Grocke, eds. 2002) adopted the Bonny Method of Guided Imagery, which involves individuals listening to classical music enabling visual images to emerge, bringing an emotional response. In my practice with clients, I have drawn on the Bonny Method and suggested that the client become aware of any image that emerges when listening to the music. At times, these images have been fearful, protective, beautiful, spiritual and loving, and are accompanied by a related emotion that emerges and is expressed. Some clients have let tears flow, others have explored an unresolved fear, such as their sense of mortality, and others feel protected by a benign being. Whatever the image, each client has been able to begin to express unresolved emotion.

For example, a young client (Crystal) who feared death listened to a piece of spiritual music she accessed on YouTube and shared how it comforted her. During the session, we played the same piece of music, and I helped her to be mindful of any images that came to mind. Once the music had stopped, in the following discussion, she described how the image of a powerful angel came to mind as if he was reaching out to her, giving her a sense of comfort and protection. Crystal shared how she was going to hold onto this image, and when she began to feel that familiar sense of fear, she would visualise that image in her mind. This goal gave her a strategy moving forward.

This type of method, when applied to music, can be effective for addressing a range of issues. For example, when working with a client who experiences angry outbursts, playing a calming and relaxing piece of music while they consciously imagine themselves in a calm, relaxed state can help prevent them from moving into an angry state. Similarly, a nervous client can listen to a dramatic piece of music and imagine themselves being confident and capable. I argue that repetition of such imagery helps to solidify change for the client.

One last point to consider in this chapter is how positive emotions can be brought about when dancing to music. As a therapist, I incorporate dancing as a regular self-care strategy every week. I believe the benefits include an in-the-moment experience where all worries and stress are left behind. Whatever the type of dance, whether it is Latin American, Ballroom, Line dancing, or Northern Soul, for the person engaging in it can bring such a sense of joy. Many dance clubs are now available for individuals to join, offering a worthwhile pastime for clients to engage in dance actively. The benefits are the enjoyment of inspiring music, active body movement, and the social aspect of making new friends. However, the dance itself can bring a genuine sense of freedom and help foster a balance between work and play.

In summary, using music in therapy can be incorporated in a variety of ways, and from a pluralistic stance, the choice of method will be decided on in collaboration with the client. The background and personal skills of the client will also be a consideration, as some will have musical skills, and others will have a particular preference for musical genres such as opera, hard rock, or pop. The therapist needs to recognise and validate the client for who they are.

References

Armstrong, C. (2015). *The therapeutic "aha!" strategies for getting your clients unstuck*. W. W. Norton. ISBN 978-0-393-70840-0

Baker, F. A., & Ballantyne, J. (2012). "You've got to accentuate the positive": Group songwriting to promote a life of enjoyment, engagement and meaning in aging Australians. *Nordic Journal of Music Therapy, 22*(1), 7–24.

Bruscia, K. E., & Grocke, D. E. (Eds.). (2002). *Guided imagery and music: The bonny method and beyond*. Barcelona Publishers.

Byrne, D. (2012). *How music works*. Canongate Books. ISBN 978-0857862501

Fairchild, R. (2018). "Everything changed when I got these drums": A collaborative case reflection. *Voices: A World Forum for Music Therapy, 18*(1), 8–10. https://doi.org/10.15845/voices.v18i1.957

Hargreaves, D. J., Miell, D., & MacDonald, R. A. R. (Eds.). (2012). *Musical imaginations*. Oxford University Press.

Holland, P. (1995). The role of music therapy in the effective use of stress. In T. Wigram, B. Saperston, & R. West (Eds.), *The art and science of music therapy: A handbook* (pp. 406–432). Harwood Academic Publishers.

Huron, D., & Marguilis, E. (2010). Musical expectancy and thrills. In P. Justin & J. Sloboda (Eds.), *Handbook of music and emotion. Theory, research and applications* (pp. 575–604). Oxford University Press.

Illie, G. & Thompson, W. F. (2011). Experiential and cognitive changes following seven minutes exposure to music and speech. *Music perception: an interdisciplinary journal. 28*(3), 247-264. ISSN: 1533-8312

Kawakami, A. I., Furukawa, K., Katahira, K., & Okanoya, K. (2013). Sad music induces pleasant emotion. *Frontiers in Psychology*, 4. https://doi.org/10.3389/fpsyg.2013.00311

Kemper, K. J., & Danhauer, S. C. (2005). Music as therapy. Featured CME Topic: Complementary and Alternative Medicine. *Southern Medical Association*, 282–288.

Leijssen, M. (2006). Validation of the body in psychotherapy. *Journal of Humanistic Psychology, 46*(2), 126–146. https://doi.org/10.1177/0022167805283782

MacDonald, R. A. R. (2013). Music, health, and well-being: A review. *International Journal of Qualitative Studies on Health and Well-Being, 8*(1), 20635. https://doi.org/10.3402/qhw.v8i0.20635doi:10.3402/qhw.v8i0.20635

Mount, N. (2018). Music therapy: Music sharing intervention with acute adolescents. *Expressive Therapies Capstone Theses*, 91. https://digitalcommons.lesley.edu/expressive_theses/91

Punkanen, M., Eerola, T., & Erkkilä, J. (2011). Biased emotional recognition in depression: Perception of emotions in music by depressed patients. *Journal of Affective Disorders, 130*(1/2), 118–126.

Särkämö, T., Tervaniemi, M., Laitinen, S., Forsblom, A., Soinila, S., Mikkonen, M., Autti, T., Silvennoinen, H. M., Erkkilä, J., Laine, M., Peretz, I., & Hietanen, M. (2008). Music listening enhances cognitive recovery and mood after middle cerebral artery stroke. *Brain, 131*(3), 866–876.

Scott, D. (2007/2008). Individual differences in response to the Bonny Method of Guided Imagery and Music. *Journal of the Association for Music and Imagery, 11*, 39–63.

Smeijsters, H. (1995). The functions of music in music therapy. In T. Wigram, B. Saperston, & R. West (Eds.), *The art and science of music therapy: A handbook* (pp. 385–394). Harwood Academic Publishers.

Taverne, E., & Nicholls, C. D. (2025). Shared music listening: Walking alongside adolescents with experiences of trauma. Brief Report: Open Access. *Counselling and Psychotherapy Research, 25*(1), 1–6.

6

Working with Objects With or Without a Sand Tray

Sand-tray therapy involves a client selecting a range of objects that can symbolise their inner experience, personal history, personal relationships, and relationship to the wider world (Fleet, 2023; Fleet et al., 2021). By arranging the objects in the sand tray, the client creates a picture representing a pressing issue for exploration. The therapist, sitting alongside, facilitates the client's exploration of the picture and uses a wide range of skills relevant to their theoretical orientation.

Lowenfeld (1993) is acknowledged to be the first professional to adopt the sand-tray and objects in therapy. Her aim was to supplement talking therapy with a visible medium that her young clients could engage with to help them express their inner experiences. Following Lowenfeld's approach, several theoretical orientations have adopted this creative way of working, including the Jungian approach (Kalff, 1980; Turner, 2005), Solution focused therapy (Taylor, 2009) and the Pluralistic approach to sand tray (Fleet, 2019, 2023; Fleet et al., 2021). However, there are differences in how each approach interprets the therapeutic process related to the theoretical underpinnings of their stance.

The Jungian approach incorporates archetypal content and symbolic processing in sand-tray work. Kalff (1980) named the Jungian sand-tray

D. Fleet, *Creative Interventions in Counselling and Psychotherapy*, Palgrave Texts in Counselling and Psychotherapy, https://doi.org/10.1007/978-3-032-16609-8_6

approach 'Sandplay' to distinguish it from Lowenfeld's work with children. Resolving unconscious conflict is the central focus of the Jungian approach. Epitomised by Kalff (2003) who argued how the client's experience is projected into the sand tray, "transferred from the inner world to the outer world and made visible" (p. 9).

Furthermore, Sandplay (Jungian) therapists view the spatial arrangement of objects in the sand tray as significant with regard to the therapeutic process. Specifically, the centre of the sand tray is viewed as highly significant, and any object placed in the centre is interpreted as an archetype of self' (Jung, 1971). Jung suggested that the psyche comprises several parts, which he labelled as archetypes, such as the persona, the mother, and the shadow, each being an inborn model of an individual's personality. Jung believed it was important for a person to dialogue with these archetypes to move towards integration and wholeness and the sand tray and objects assist the client to engage in deep discovery. Turner, another Sandplay therapist and researcher (2008), suggested how objects are brought to the centre later on in the process, as a move towards healing, indicating progression.

A gestalt approach to using the sand tray in therapy can be described as a "simple form of experimentation" (Stevens, 2004, p. 2). Stevens (2004) discussed how sand-tray work helps clients to overcome resistance. By engaging in the creative process, adult clients can overcome blocks to the therapeutic process such as having a tendency to intellectualise, avoiding expression of emotion. The symbolic objects help a client to shift to a more open, spontaneous and creative attitude when exploring and expressing their issues and move towards healing.

A person-centred therapist adopting sand-tray work will prioritise the client's innate capacity to solve their own problems (Rogers, 1957). In this approach, the therapist will aim to offer the core conditions of unconditional positive regard, empathy and congruency (Merry, 1999; Rogers, 1957). The therapist will avoid making any interpretations on the meaning of the symbolic objects used by the client so as to avoid establishing a power imbalance. Woodhouse (2008) suggested how Polanyi's (1958) term of 'indwelling' describes how the PC therapist aims to enter the client's world, staying close to the client's frame of reference as they experience the sand-tray process.

A stark warning concerning the psychoanalyst, Edna O'Shauhnessy, working from her own agenda and projecting her own preconceptions onto the client was highlighted by Michael Bacon (2024, https://aeon.co/essays-dismal-years-in-psychoanalysis-with-melaie-kleins-disiple retrieved 13 May 2025).

Bacon warns how a therapist's theoretical indoctrination, along with an inward-looking approach, when dogma overrides sound judgement regarding the therapeutic relationship and when conceptualising the client, can result in harm to the client.

Bacon discovered essays written by the psychoanalyst Edna O'Shaughnessy. In three of those essays, he recognised that she was referring to him as a young boy receiving treatment from her. Bacon communicates how she viewed and analysed him through a "distorted lens of Kleinian theory" (Bacon, 2024, p. 4) and described her use of him to "play out already fixed ideas" (Bacon, 2024, p. 18).

Bacon also shared how he was impacted by how O'Shaughnessy communicated her dislike of him as a young boy, using adjectives such as nasty, self-pitying, and manipulative to describe him in her essays. Such a misrepresentation of his character resulted in Bacon experiencing a sense of violation. However, Bacon's resilience and self-awareness appeared to help him fight back, sparing him permanent harm. However, in a therapeutic relationship when the client is experiencing severe distress, it can be difficult for them to challenge such misrepresentations and damaging assessments, especially regarding the power imbalance. The risk is that the client could experience long-term damage to their self-concept.

Acknowledging the client's perspective and strengths is vital to being aware of such an imbalance of power in the therapeutic relationship. Furthermore, a therapeutic relationship based on acceptance and collaboration between therapist and client can help guard against the therapist assuming such a superior and possibly abusive position.

A solution focused therapist using sand-tray work would aim to move the client's attention away from a problem and focus on the client's strengths in order to develop coping skills. The sand-tray therapy will be structured, with the therapist asking questions involving exceptions to the problem. Scaling is also a prominent feature that involves rating problems from 1–10 or 1–100 to indicate how significant the issue is as perceived by the client. Taylor (2009) based on the "Miracle Question" (Macdonald, 2007) suggests to the client that they create a picture in the sand, to illustrate "how their world would look if the problem did not exist" (Fleet, 2023, p. 7). The aim here is to help the client adopt a more positive position as they find ways to move forward.

The foundation for pluralistic sand-tray therapy (PSTT) (Fleet, 2019, 2023; Fleet et al., 2021) is based on the pluralistic approach initially established by Cooper and McLeod (2007). It is founded on humanistic principles that emphasise the 'client as an active agent of change' (Cooper & McLeod, 2011). Acknowledging the client's unique way of being and personal autonomy is central to the approach, which is synonymous with the humanistic tradition (Cooper & McLeod, 2011). Therefore, the pluralistic therapist will work collaboratively with the client throughout the therapeutic process. McLeod (2018) argued how dialogical communication, utilising the client's input and the therapist's knowledge, is a "helpful and healing experience in itself" (p. 49). Furthermore, the understanding that different clients need different things in therapy at different times supports the pluralistic practice of drawing on various therapeutic approaches (Cooper & McLeod, 2011).

As a pluralistic therapist, I adapt my sand-tray therapy approach to suit the client. Sometimes, a client will want a more structured approach, with the therapist suggesting what to depict in the sand tray. For example, if a client is experiencing a dilemma and has to decide between two options, I might suggest that they split the sand tray in half and choose objects to represent both decisions. Then, I would help them explore each decision's positive and negative repercussions along with the associated thoughts and emotions of making each decision. This process can give a clearer picture, helping the client in the decision-making process.

In comparison, for a client who presents with a less specific issue and, for example, states, "I feel so down, but I'm not sure why", I would suggest that they work in a non-structured way. Here, I would guide them to look at the objects to see what 'jumps out' to them and place them in the sand. This way of working can help the client begin to explore experiences that are out of awareness at that time, and as they engage in the creative process using symbolic objects, insight and understanding, as well as emotional expression, often occurs.

Case Study: Shirley—A Client-Participant of Pluralistic Sand-Tray Therapy

Shirley was a client-participant in my multiple case study (Fleet, 2019, 2023; Fleet et al., 2021) using PSTT and she communicated two goals in her initial session. The first goal was to be able to manage her panic attacks, and the second was to speak about something she had not spoken out loud before (2019). As the therapist-researcher, I believed that an adapted CBT strategy involving using the body, imagination and breathing when Shirley's panic began to build might help her begin to manage her panic attacks. I suggested this to her, and Shirley was happy to 'give it a go' (Fleet, 2019, 2023).

We worked together to decide the most appropriate breathing strategy, with me offering possible suggestions. Shirley shared how she experienced her panic building in her chest, and I suggested that she place her hand on her chest as she imagined her panic (Shirley's choice, her panic as a red colour) moving up her body and breathing this out of her mouth. She then imagined a light blue healing energy (again Shirley's own choice of colour), breathing this in through her nose and moving down to her chest, mixing with her panic (Fleet, 2023, p. 18). Shirley then continued to engage in this strategy until the panic began to fade, and she practised this regularly in between therapy sessions. Shirley's feedback was positive, as she felt more in control of her panic, and she shared how she would continue to use this strategy even when therapy had come to an end.

For Shirley's goal of speaking the unspoken, she was happy to use the sand tray and objects to help her voice this unexpressed issue. In the initial session, I had asked Shirley if there was anything she could tell me to help her do that, and she responded by saying she would like me to ask her questions.

This specific request was helpful to me as her therapist, as she approved my active presence in her process. In addition, I believe it helped to equalise the power balance somewhat, as she took the lead by making this request.

Shirley selected a Russian doll in one session and placed it in the sand (Fleet, 2019, p. 114). She observed this object for a while without speaking. After some time, I said, "I wonder how it would be to open that and pull out the other parts and place them in the sand?" After a few moments, Shirley began to take the Russian doll apart and placed the different parts in the sand in a line, from largest to smallest. Then, after a few moments of silence, she began to speak:

Shirley: "It's like I am living a lie"
Doreen: "Mmm"
(Few moments of silence.)
Shirley: "It's like…something has to happen to want to say it because…erm"
Doreen: "You don't want to say it?"
Shirley: "No"
Doreen: "It's hard to say?"
Shirley: "That erm…religion is not real"
Doreen: "Religion?"
Shirley: "No…no…not religion…but God"

(Fleet, 2019, pp. 114–115).

Shirley came from a family with strict religious beliefs and strong expectations that 'as our daughter, you must believe in God'. This cultural expectation weighed heavily on Shirley, and her questioning of the belief in God had to remain a secret as she did not want to be ostracised by her family. The only place she felt free to voice her questioning of her family's blind belief in God had been in the therapy room, and this brought her much relief. The symbolic objects and the questions and reflections I asked helped Shirley speak the unspoken.

Case Study: Josh

In the initial session, Josh described issues throughout his life that made him feel that he did not belong. Similar to one of Shirley's goals, his goal for therapy was to talk about things he had not spoken of before and, express his feelings,

"To feel it...the pain...I always push it down".

As Josh's therapist, I responded by informing him that I would do my best to help him achieve the task of expressing his pain and reflected on how it seemed like he had decided that it was the right time for him to unpack his pain. Josh nodded in agreement and stated that he wanted me to take an active part in the sessions and not just sit in silence throughout, which would make him feel awkward. I reassured him that I saw the therapeutic relationship as a two-way process and that I would engage and respond to him.

Josh went on to share how, as a young boy, he knew he was different from the other boys in school and how his father forced him to play football, which he hated and in his words:

> "I was terrible at it".

Josh then looked around the room and commented on the sand tray and objects, saying,

> "Oh, do you work with children?"

I replied, "Sometimes therapists use sand trays and objects with children, but I use them with adult clients who want to work creatively in that way. The objects serve as physical metaphors, helping clients talk about thoughts and feelings they find difficult to express, and Josh replied,

> "Sounds interesting...I've always been creative...love drawing and painting"

In response to his statement, I suggested to Josh that he could work creatively in the sessions, such as drawing, painting, or using the objects in a sand tray. Josh was very interested and began to ask questions about using the sand tray, which I answered. I also shared examples of how the objects can act as physical metaphors (Fleet, 2023, p. 75), representing personal experience.

Near the end of the initial appointment, Josh decided he would like to try the sand-tray method.

Image 6.1 Josh's sand-tray image in his first session

In the first therapy session, Josh placed an object in the sand of a hunched-over figure (Image 6.1) and placed other objects facing it and said,

> "That's me, there…curled up…when I was a kid, sometimes I wished they would all just disappear. My bedroom and my music was my safety."

I helped Josh to explore his thoughts and feelings of being different, judged, and lonely. He shared how he always felt judged,

> "I never belonged, I felt they hated me because I was not like them. Not a typical lad, Dad hated me for that, always trying to toughen me up".

We explored his sense of being hated and Josh was able to allow the tears to come without stopping them. A little later in the session he shared:

> "When I was fourteen, I knew I liked boys, I had a cousin who was a few years older, she knew, this is her (picked up the cat) Stella (pseudonym) she understood, she was the only one who understood. I could talk to her but didn't see her often, she lived in the next town.

> Anyway, I had a big argument with Dad when I was about sixteen and it all came out. I told them I was gay and he just stood there, frozen...didn't say a word...just had this disgusted look on his face" (picked up the monster figure and placed it back down in the sand). Mum looked after me though, tried to make him listen but he never accepted it, after that he hardly spoke to me".
> In later sessions, Josh described how his mother (represented by the object in a robe (Madonna) had tried her best with his Dad to get him to understand but it never happened.

The objects serving as powerful symbols of Josh's pain aided his expression of his previous guarded experience and unresolved emotion linked to his past. In a later session, Josh shared more about his terrible experience at school being bullied and the objects of the three-headed dog and the witch representing those bullies who made his experience at school unbearable at times. By the end of therapy, Josh had achieved his goal of expressing the deep pain stemming from his childhood, bringing much relief. He was also able to move to a place of self-compassion stating,

> "When I think back to that little boy...I feel so sorry that I went through that...I am a good person, always was...now I have a partner who loves me".

In addition to expressing his previously unresolved pain, Josh also achieved a phenomenological shift in his "inner world perceptions of I think, I feel, I believe, I am" (Fleet, 2023, p. 38) by offering self-compassion. He was able to shift his focus from the pain he experienced as a child with the internalised message, 'I am in pain', to seeing this in his past, and offering tenderness to the child within helped him move towards healing. This phenomenological shift also involved Josh now being able to see how strong he was, even as a young boy. Although there had been much pressure for him to act differently and fit in, he never compromised, and although it had been a painful journey, he was proud of that. He had shifted in his perception of seeing himself as a wounded boy to a fighter. Despite the bullying and harsh treatment, he stayed true to himself.

Specific Advantages When Using Objects and Sand Trays in Therapy

There are specific advantages to using objects and sand trays in therapy, including touch, the spatial arrangement of objects, moving and removing objects, burying objects in the sand, and manipulating the sand in the tray, which contributes to the therapeutic process (Fleet, 2019, 2023, p. 51).

Touch

Montague (1971) described how touch "was the authentic voice of feeling" (p. 287). The issue of touch in therapy has often been associated with risk, as a therapist touching a client might be construed as crossing a boundary, and safe boundaries are required so that the client feels safe in the therapeutic context (Fleet, 2023). However, when using a sand tray and/or objects, the client can benefit from the process of touch, as they touch the sand and/or objects without crossing any boundaries. Markell (2002) suggests that when a client smooths the sand with their hand or holds an object, it establishes a dialogue between the client's internal and external experience that links the psyche and the physical.

Furthermore, Homeyer and Sweeney (2011) stated, "It's almost as if the touching of the sand facilitated the loosening of the tongue" (p. 32). Hass-Cohen (2008) suggests how working creatively using touch and vision helps to process emotions and contributes to therapeutic change.

Many clients touch the sand as they speak. This might involve smoothing the sand, pinching the grains between their fingers, or digging holes, which can be self-soothing behaviour, helping them manage any anxiety as well as beginning to engage with the sand tray (Fleet, 2023). Therefore, the physical act of touching the sand can be a helpful action, aiding the therapeutic process in face-to-face sand-tray therapy, with the therapist providing the sand tray.

Badenoch (2008) describes how a person touching the sand facilitates a process whereby the sensation of touch moves "from the fingers up to the thalamus, then to the parietal lobe in the brain, associated with touch" (p. 12). Then the act of offering empathy by the therapist, helps the client to begin to explore and express their pain. Badenoch (2008) argued how this process results in "new synapses which carry that information throughout the brain and blood flow changes course to more smoothing paths" (p. 12) bringing relief to the client. De Little's (2020) stance is in line with Badenoch's supporting the link between biology and emotional regulations.

Moving Objects

When the client physically moves the objects around the sand tray or mirroring an action with an object alone, can result in a powerful 'here and now' enactment of an experience. For example, Jackie, a client-participant in my case study research (2019), regularly moved objects around the sand tray. Jackie was living with a married man, and although he had not been happy before meeting Jackie, she was fearful he would end the relationship and move back in with his wife. In one session, Jackie chose a decorative egg object to represent herself, a pink quartz heart to represent her partner and a Pinocchio object to represent her partner's wife. Then, Jackie placed a small piece of train track into the sand and positioned the decorative egg (her) at one end and Pinocchio (partner's wife) at the other end. As Jackie explored her fear, she continued to move the pink quartz heart (her partner) up and down the track. This physical act appeared to help Jackie to express and unpack her fear, the projection not only being verbal and emotional but physically emphasising expression in the present.

Spatial Arrangement

The spatial arrangement of objects placed in the sand by a client can help the client unpack the quality of those relationships (Fleet, 2023). For example, a client might place an object in the centre of the sand tray representing them and then arrange objects representing significant people in their lives. For example, if one parent is placed close to the object representing self, this might indicate a close relationship.

Contrary, if an object representing the other parent is at a distance, this might represent a relationship that is not so close. This visual picture can help the client express the closeness of one parent and, in contrast, the distance experienced in the other relationship along with the associated emotions.

Removing and Burying Objects Using a Sand-Tray

Similarly, removing and burying objects can help the client explore as the physical action can bring a past experience to the 'here and now' for processing. A client burying an object in the sand can have different meanings for different clients. For example, an abusive person in the client's life might be depicted and being buried beneath the sand might represent a wish that they are no longer in the client's life. Alternatively, an object might be pushed into the sand, representing someone or something that is unmovable, the client communicating how they want them or it to remain in their life. For example, John, a client-participant in my research study (Fleet, 2019, p. 229, 2023, p. 58) pushed an object of a pig representing his dog into the sand, with just its head visible. He had experienced losses, and he demonstrated the love he still had: his love for his dog by saying, "She's not going anywhere" (Fleet, 2019, p. 229, 2023, p. 58).

Using Objects in Online Therapy

In my practice, clients have often used objects that have a significant meaning for them, both in face-to-face and online therapy. For example, childhood toys can help a client link to unresolved feelings from their past. Such expressions can bring relief, helping them to express emotions such as hurt, sadness and anger. For example, objects representing the death of a sibling, a parent or a grandparent may remind the client of the pain of that loss. Furthermore, exploring a loss can bring a sense of connectedness concerning the love they had for the deceased.

For example, Amara, a female client, came to therapy to talk about her grief relating to the loss of her mother, who had died three months before Amara's wedding. As she began to talk about her grief, Amara held on to her mother's wedding ring, which she wore on a chain around her neck. Touching her mother's ring appeared to help Amara talk about her loss and her feelings about how unfair it was that her mother was taken away from her so close to her wedding. Amara was a religious person and believed in the afterlife. In a later session, she shared that wearing the ring made her feel connected to her mother,

> "Knowing she is always with me, helps me, I can feel her presence sometimes".

The idea of using objects to manage anxiety has existed for several years. Winnicott (1971) coined the term 'transitional object' (TO) to refer to an infant who holds an object such as a teddy bear, described as the "first 'not-me' possession (p. 1). Winnicott saw this as a healthy process, with the TO standing for the mother's breast. As the separation process begins, a TO, such as a teddy bear, can be a defence against anxiety and help the infant fall asleep. Modell (1968), in line with Winnicott, suggested how TOs aid self-soothing against anxiety for an individual.

Such TOs can be helpful when a client is exploring childhood issues such as abuse, neglect, and abandonment. The process of touch can help them connect to the child within and unpack unexpressed pain.

In summary, using objects with or without a sand tray can help clients explore past, present, and future issues and their inner world experience, which causes them distress. Furthermore, the advantages of the symbolic process and touch can help a client access unexpressed emotions and deep-rooted painful experiences that need to be processed for healing to occur. The creative process involves the client physically touching the objects and/or sand with their hands and visually observing the picture, which results in an externalising process. This process helps the client avoid becoming overwhelmed by their pain as they project their emotions onto the objects, and such externalising "with definite boundaries facilitates the client to stay with their pain" (Fleet, 2023, pp. 57,

58). Additionally, offering structured or unstructured guidance helps meet a client's particular needs, whether in face-to-face therapy or online.

Note: For a more in depth consideration of pluralistic sand-tray therapy, please refer to my text Pluralistic Sand-Tray therapy. (Fleet, D. (2023). *Pluralistic sand-tray therapy. Humanistic principles for working creatively with adult clients.* London & New York: Routledge, Taylor & Francis Group. ISBN:978-0-367-74774-9.

References

Bacon, M. (2024). *The therapist who hated me. My dismal years in psychoanalysis with Melanie Klein's disciple* (Ed. Pam Weintraub). Aaeon Essays. https://aeon.co/essays-dismal-years-in-psychoanalysis-with-melanie-klein-disiple, retrieved 13 May, 2025.

Badenoch, B. (2008). *Being a brain-wise therapist: A practical guide to interpersonal neurobiology.* W. W. Norton.

Cooper, M., & McLeod, J. (2007). A pluralistic framework for counselling and psychotherapy: Implications for research. *Counselling and Psychotherapy Research, 7*(3), 135–143. http://eprints.edlr.strath.ac.uk/5213/

Cooper, M., & McLeod, J. (2011). *Pluralistic counselling and psychotherapy.* Sage.

De Little, M. M. (2020). Using the sand-tray in the context of the latest research in neuroscience to transform clients' defences. *Canadian Journal of Counselling and Psychotherapy, 54*(1), 1–26, vii.

Fleet, D. (2019). *Transformation hidden in the sand: Developing a theoretical framework using a sand-tray intervention with adult clients* (Doctoral thesis). Staffordshire University. Stoke-on-Trent. Available from Ethos STORE—Staffordshire Online Repository. https://eprints.staffs.ac.uk/id/eprint/5763

Fleet. D. Reeves. A., Burton, A., & DasGupta, M. P. (2021). Transformation hidden in the sand: A pluralistic theoretical framework using sand-tray with adult clients. First published online (14 June, 2021). *Journal of Creativity in Mental Health.* https://doi.org/10.1080/15401383.2021.1936738

Fleet, D. (2023). *Pluralistic sand-tray therapy. Humanistic principles for working creatively with adult clients.* Routledge, Taylor & Francis Group. ISBN:978-0-367-74774-9.
Hass-Cohen, N. (2008). CREATE: Art therapy relational neuroscience principles (ATR-N). In N. Hass-Cohen & R. Carr (Eds.), *Art therapy and clinical neuroscience.* Jessica Kingsley Publishers.
Homeyer, L. E., & Sweeney, D. S. (2011). *Sandtray therapy: A practical manual* (2nd ed.). Routledge.
Jung, C. G. (1971). The archetypes and the collective unconscious. In H. Read, M. Fordham, G. Adler, & W. McGuire (Eds.), (R. F. C. Hull, Trans.), *Collected works of C. G. Jung* (Vol. 9.1). Princeton University Press (Original work published in 1934).
Kalff, D. M. (1980). *Sandplay.* Sigo Press.
Kalff, D. (2003). *Sandplay: A psychotherapeutic approach to the psyche.* Cloverdale, CA: Temenos Press.
Lowenfeld. M. (1993). *Understanding children's sandplay: Lowenfeld's world technique.* Antony Rowe Ltd.
Macdonald, A. (2007). *Solution -focused therapy: Theory, research & practice.* Sage.
Markell, M. J. (2002). *Sand, water, silence: The embodiment of spirit, explorations in matter and psyche.* Jessica Kingsley Publishers.
McLeod, J. (2018). *Pluralistic therapy: Distinctive features.* Routledge, Taylor & Francis Group.
Merry, T. (1999). *Learning and being in person-centred counselling.* PCCS Books.
Modell, A. (1968). *Object love and reality.* International Universities Press Inc.
Montague, A. (1971). *Touching: The human significance of the skin.* Harper & Row.
Polanyi, M. (1958). *Personal knowledge; Towards a post-critical philosophy.* University of Chicago Press.
Rogers, C. R. (1957). The necessary and sufficient conditions of therapeutic personality change. *Journal of Consulting Psychology, 21*, 95–103.
Stevens, C. (2004). Playing in the sand. *The British Gestalt Journal, 13*(1), 18–23. http://www.psychotherapynottingham.com/Pages/Playing_in_th_Sand.html
Taylor, E. R. (2009). Sandtray and solution-focused therapy. *International Journal of Play Therapy, 18*(1), 56–68.
Turner, B. A. (2005). *The handbook of sandplay therapy.* Temenos Press.

Winnicott, D. W. (1971).Transitional objects and transitional phenomena. In D.W.Winnicott (Ed.), *Playing and reality* (pp. 1–25). Tavistock.

Woodhouse, J. (2008). SANDPLAY: Growing ground in person-centred play therapy. Chapter 4. In S. Keys & T. Walshaw (Eds.), *Person-centred work with children and young people: UK practitioner perspectives* (pp. 29–38). PCCS Books Ltd.

7

Working with Dreams

Humankind has been fascinated by dreams throughout history and across cultures, and despite extensive research, there is much still to understand. Ruby, P. M. (2011) stated, "Dreaming is still a mystery of human cognition, although it has been studied experimentally for more than a century" (2011, p. 1). Within counselling and psychotherapy, various theoretical approaches have offered their understanding and methods of working with a client's dreams. However, continuous debate still exists into the nature and function of dreams, with researchers providing arguments based on their underpinning theoretical beliefs. Questions on whether dreams are linked to consciousness, hallucinations, memory insertions or imaginative experiences that are 'subject to the will' and a consequence of unconscious authorship (Ichikawa, 2009; McGinn, 2004) have continued to fascinate researchers for several years with the debate showing no sign of abating.

Sigmund Freud (1900, 1910, 1922, 1953) and Carl Jung (1961, 1965, 1974, 1984) were two pioneering theorists who offered their perspectives on the nature and function of dreams. Although they both viewed dreams as significant in connecting to the unconscious, they had contrasting views on the nature of dreams and dream interpretation.

D. Fleet, *Creative Interventions in Counselling and Psychotherapy*, Palgrave Texts in Counselling and Psychotherapy, https://doi.org/10.1007/978-3-032-16609-8_7

Freud's (1910) stance centred on his belief that dreams are a manifestation of repressed desires, unfulfilled wishes and issues of sexuality or childhood conflicts. In contrast, Jung (1961) viewed dreams as essential tools, providing insight contributing to 'individuation' and future personal growth. Jung's concept of individuation (1959) concerns the individual in the process of self discovery and realisation, leading to psychological integration, becoming whole. For example, such personal development may involve the person no longer conforming to external expectations. Their growth might involve such change that they move away from operating behind a social mask and are now able to function in a more congruent manner. Jung suggested that "if we paid serious attention to dreams, they would reveal practical and important hints about where the unconscious was leading the dreamer" (Van De Castle, 1994, pp. 157–158).

Horton (2020), a contemporary author on dreams, defined dreaming as "the recollection of mental content from sleep" (p. 1) that can be "fragmented, brief, non-narrative, thought-like, which can contain emotion, sometimes having no complex plot" (p. 1). This broader explanation of dreams accounts for the contradistinction of dreams; sometimes, they have a straightforward narrative, and yet, at other times, they contain a confusing set of features. How often have you heard someone say, "I had such a strange dream, so bizarre, nothing made sense, everything was so disconnected"?

Furthermore, Walker (2009) argued how most spontaneously recalled dream reports occur in REM sleep (rapid eye movement). However, Solms (2000) suggested how the dreamer can recall dreams from non-REM sleep.

Many researchers and therapists hold to the assertion that dreams have an adaptive value. The author Joan Harthan who has been working with dreams for over twenty five years, suggests how, "dreams provide a powerful path to self-awareness" (2013, p. 3) and places value on how dreams can access material that we are not consciously aware of. Hartham's ardour on the usefulness of dreams and how dreams can "offer creative solutions to problems" is clearly apparent in her writing, with her stating, "Peace and happiness we all seek is attainable. You'll find the signposts in your dreams, all you have to do is stay on the road" (2013, p. 4).

Lucid Dreaming

A distinctive type of dreaming is lucid dreaming, "when we become aware that one is dreaming while dreaming" (Baird et al., 2019. p. 305). Van Eeden (1913) wrote about his own lucid dreams and described how he reached a state of perfect awareness. Other researchers (Dresler et al, 2011; LaBerge, 2015; Windt, 2015) supported Van Eeden's accounts of how a person can be physiologically asleep yet aware they are dreaming and can sometimes adopt active intention during the dream. LaBerge et al. (1981) asked lucid dreamers to move their eyes in up-down or left–right movements as soon as they were aware they were lucid dreaming, objectively verifying lucid dreaming.

Case Study: Naomi

In her initial appointment, Naomi shared that she did not see herself as religious but as spiritual, believing in the transpersonal:

> "I just think that we are far more than the body and mind…I do believe that we are a spirit in a body, and when we die, our spirit leaves the body. Energy can't disappear; it just changes."

In one session, Naomi shared a lucid dream stating:

> "I was awake, I knew I was dreaming… I was fully aware. It was like I was flying and I knew, someone…sort of like a higher being was with me. Sort of flying just above me but I couldn't see them but I knew they were there. They were guiding me to places and when I looked down there was so much violence…so much horror. I couldn't move my gaze away as much as I tried to resist looking at all this horror. As it went on I got angry and shouted in a very loud voice, 'THIS IS NOT REAL'
> As soon as I shouted this, I felt an immense relief and opened my eyes, but I didn't awake…I was already awake".

As Naomi's therapist, it was essential that I respected her spiritual beliefs and I helped her unpack her dream, and by asking her purposeful questions and helping her to reflect deeply, we could focus on the various elements of the dream, the symbols representing meaning. Harthan (2013) stated how "dreams use metaphorical language to tell their stories and employ symbolism as a means of expressing complex ideas and thoughts" (p. 7).

At the end of the session, Naomi's understanding was that she had been tested in some way. She shared,

> "The violence, the horror was just a perspective, and once I could see this truth, the horror was gone."

I believe it was crucial that I stayed with Naomi's point of reference and did not give my interpretation of what I thought the dream meant or did not mean. For Naomi, this dream was special, and she believed that, in some way, she had connected with a higher realm, bringing an opportunity for her to grow.

Bulkeley (1995) suggested how such spiritual dreams bring the individual closer to the sacred, guiding waking life, which was the case for Naomi.

I would advocate respecting a client's perspective even if it contrasts with your own; after all, what proof is there that Naomi's belief is wrong? Furthermore, is the process of determining what is right and what is wrong relevant in this context?

Dreamwork with the Bereaved

Dreamwork with the bereaved can be a valuable creative intervention, helping them to come to terms with their loss. LoConto (1998) argued how a bereaved person dreaming of a deceased loved one can facilitate the grieving process. Mallon (2026) argued how dreams "can be used in bereavement care as a starting point to address emotional aspects of loss" (2005, p. 43). Dreams related to the death of a loved one, can help the bereaved to accept their love one is deceased and help the person express their emotions in waking life (Mallon, 2026).

Many bereaved people experience vivid dreams involving the presence of the deceased. Wright et al. (2014) suggested that such dreams can be pleasant although sometimes disturbing. These researchers argued how common dream themes included pleasant past memories, the deceased being free of illness, the deceased now in the afterlife appearing to be at peace and the deceased communicating a message (Wright et al., 2014, p. 132). Such dreams helped individuals to accept the death of a loved one, brought comfort, enhanced their belief in spirituality, but for some, resulted in feelings of sadness (Wright et al., 2014). The outcome of Wright et al.'s study (2014) suggested that dreaming of the deceased when there was a loving relationship was deeply meaningful for the bereaved. Elisabeth Kubler-Ross (1975) suggested that dreaming of a deceased loved one is a true contact emerging from the spiritual plane.

Case Study: Natalie's Dream of her Deceased Grandfather

Natalie came to therapy because she was struggling after the break up of her relationship. She had lived with her ex-partner for three years and was now in the flat they had shared, living alone. Natalie had explored her loneliness in several sessions, and although she had quite a good social life due to a close circle of friends, her loneliness was most acute when she came back home to her flat. In one session, she discussed her desire to get a dog and began making plans. While working, her parents agreed that they would look after the dog when she was at work and encouraged her to get one. A few weeks later, in another session, she shared a lucid dream:

> "I had the most lovely dream, my grandad appeared to me carrying a little white puppy, handed it over to me and said, 'here's Rosie'. I couldn't tell what type of dog it was because it was so small, but when I get one, I will definitely call it Rosie."

I asked Natalie how she felt about that dream, and she shared how real it seemed as if she'd had a real visit from her grandad. There was no need to explore it any further because Natalie had her own beliefs about what the dream meant.

About three weeks later, Natalie was searching on the internet looking at dogs for sale and came across a small white puppy. In the next session, she shared:

> "I just knew it was Rosie. I contacted the breeder straight away, and now Rosie is home. She has made such a difference to me. I love her so much. I believe Grandad helped me out. I know he is watching over me."

Natalie's belief concerning her grandad contacting her from the afterlife had an extremely positive impact on her; it was so important to respect and acknowledge her beliefs.

Gestalt Dreamwork

Gestalt therapy was founded by Fritz Perls (1873–1930) and his partner Laura Perls (1905–1990). Perls (In Fagan and I. Shepherd, 1970) argued that a dream is an existential message with every element being a part of the dreamer.

The task of a gestalt therapist "is to help their clients to experience repressed, ambivalent, and unpleasant things in order to accept and implement them in their whole self" (Holzinger et al., 2021, p. 1220). Therefore, the idea of 'unfinished business and seeking closure is a central feature (Perls et al., 1995).

In Gestalt dream work, the dreamer plays an active role (Gegenfurtner, 2005). Each character or symbol in the dream is a message from the unconscious, thought to represent an aspect of the dreamer (Holzinger et al., 2021). Another central feature of this approach to working with dreams is to aid the client in exploring their dream "through their bodily sensations" in addition to their thoughts (Perls, 1992, p. 4931).

Pluralistic Strategy as an Adaptation of Gestalt Dreamwork

Holzinger et al. (2021) conducted a study based on the Gestalt dreamwork approach that embraced all the senses. This strategy involved various stages that involved asking the dreamer to tell their dream in the first person as if they were dreaming in the present, speak as the dream character as if it was a play on the stage, choose two main dream characters who were in conflict and speak from each perspective. Throughout the process, it was important for the dreamer to communicate their feelings throughout the exercise and, near the end, to explore what they wanted to do next (Holzinger et al, 2021).

I found adapting this Gestalt strategy to a pluralistic approach quite straightforward. Firstly, the dreamer's active participation in Gestalt is compatible with the pluralistic approach, which views collaboration between therapist and client as essential to the therapeutic process. Furthermore, the Gestalt therapist asks questions and asking dialogical questions (McLeod, 2018) is a feature of the pluralistic approach, aiding the client engage in deeper reflection.

The following case study demonstrates how a pluralistic therapist could engage in this approach to dream work.

Case Study: Sam's Dream Work

Sam, a woman receiving therapy, had explored her childhood of being abandoned by her mother, growing up in foster care, and moving from one home to another. After eight weeks of receiving therapy, Sam shared a short dream she had had. Van de Castle (1994) suggested how "very short dreams or dream fragments can also be profitably pursued with a gestalt approach" (p. 193).

My own pluralistic stance to working with a client's dreams involves an adaptation of the gestalt approach.

Sam stated,

> "This dream…it was strange. I was standing next to a swamp I couldn't see beneath its muddy surface. I watched as I saw a dog struggling, trying to crawl out of the swamp."

At this point, it was essential that I ask Sam if she wanted me to help her work on her dream and make sense of it, as in pluralistic therapy, the client is involved in any decision-making process.

Sam was happy to work in this way, so I suggested that one way of working with a dream is based on the belief that each character or symbol in the dream can relate to an aspect of themselves. If she wanted, we could work that way. Sam was enthusiastic about trying this strategy and seeing if she could make sense of her dream.

The following communication took place:

Therapist (T.) "So you have three symbols in your dream, you watching, the dog and the swamp itself. So tell me about the dog, as if it was you, use the words 'I' or 'Me' and talk in the present as if the dream was happening now".

Sam (S) "Okay, me as the dog, I am trying to get away, desperate to get away.

(T) "How does it feel trying to get away?

(S) "Struggling and scared, sad…I feel sad…it's me trying to get away…but nobody is there to help. I have to do it on my own…like always"

(T) "You always have to do it on your own… always helping others but they don't help you"

(S) "Mmm…I'm a people pleaser…faithful little dog..that's me, give me a pat on my head"

(T) "Always trying to make others happy?"

(S) "Yeah…but…getting sick of it…I need to be noticed too"

(T) "How does that feel wanting to be noticed?"

(S) "I'm fed up""

(PAUSE)

(T) "Okay…shall we move to the swamp now?

(S) "(mmm…yeah)

(T) "So tell me about the swamp, as if you are the swamp and again talk by using the words 'I' or 'Me'.

(S) "I am dark, slimy, a greeny-black, you can't see beneath my surface. I have secrets".

(T) "What do you want to say to the dog?"

(S) "Think you can escape do you…you are weak"

(T) "What does the dog reply?"

(S) "I am going…got nothing to lose"
(T) "What do you as the dog need to do now?"
(S) "You (the swamp) can't keep me here. Need to be strong, speak up for God's sake, say No!
(T) "What are you feeling in your body right now?
(S) "I feel heavy in my stomach, I need to get away…don't want to be in that swamp"
(PAUSE)
[I asked Sam the questions above to help her engage in deeper reflection]
(T) "Shall we move onto you as the watcher now?
(S) "Yeah"
(T) "So tell me about the watcher. You, watching the dog trying to escape, and watching the swamp. Again use the word 'I' or 'Me' as if the dream is happening right now."
(S) "I am watching. It's like a battle between the dog and the swamp. They are fighting against each other. The dog wanting to escape, the swamp keeping hold"

Dual Reflection (T & S) Following the Dream Strategy

The two-way conversation, with myself as therapist and Sam, involved us summarising what came out during the dream exercise. We agreed that the dog symbol represented her as a 'people pleaser'. Her abandonment and unstable childhood had an impact on her trying to behave in a way that would prevent people from leaving her or sending her away. The lake seemed to represent events from her past that she could not let go of, which fed into her putting her own needs to one side, resulting in her being taken advantage of in her relationships. The symbol of her as the watcher seemed to correlate with her trying to find a way to change by observing the things that still brought her distress.

I asked Sam what she needed to do now to bring about change, and she responded,

"I think I need to begin to think about my own needs as well as others and start saying No to them sometimes".

Assessment—Asking Sam What it Was Like Taking Part in the Dreamwork Process

This final part of the strategy was important for Sam to be able to give feedback and for me, as her therapist and this occurred not only through formal feedback at the end of therapy but also via "ongoing metatherapeutic dialogue (Papayianni & Cooper, 2017) defined as "the dialogue between therapist and client on the nature of therapeutic work and the means by which it can be of greatest help to clients" (p. 1). The client's feedback enables the therapist to address anything that the client found unhelpful in this dreamwork session. Sam gave feedback and shared:

"It did feel strange at first being the things in my dream, but I did get into it, and in the end, I think it helped me. Also, your questions helped me to talk and get into it. When we talked about it afterwards, I felt it helped me think about changes I need to make. I really need to stop being that people-pleaser".

The dream work appeared to have a lasting impact on Sam, and she continued to discuss it in the following two sessions when she explored how to bring change to her relationships. She also shared how she felt she had talked about her abandonment enough, and now she needed to let go of this aspect of her past and move on. She said,

"I am stopping trying to make someone stay in my life because always trying to please them makes me so tired. If they don't want to stay with me, then so be it".

Staying with this theme of change, we worked on her personal boundaries, and she began to set rules about how she could keep herself safe and happy in relationships. I also worked on helping her say the word 'NO' when she needed to, which had previously been non-existent in past relationships. At the end of therapy, Sam was committed to changing her life and making deeper connections with others where she could establish 'give and take' in future relationships.

Group Dream Workshop

During my time as a counselling and psychotherapy trainer, I regularly facilitated a group dream workshop for students. A facilitator can take various approaches, but I adopted a Gestalt-type workshop.

In advance I asked the students four weeks prior to the session to begin recording their dreams and to bring one to work with. I also prepared a small powerpoint to summarise some of the main points of this approach concerning:

- Gestalt dreamwork is based on the belief that each character or symbol in the dream can relate to an aspect of themselves.
- The dreamer plays an active role in the dream work.
- Each character or symbol in the dream is thought to be a message from the unconscious.
- Be aware that material emerging from the unconscious might stimulate uncomfortable emotions linked to material that has not been experienced fully or at all.

At this point, I made sure that myself (an experienced trainer, therapist and supervisor) would be available to offer support. In addition, I had another tutor also available as extra support if needed.

I had also prepared a handout to be handed to the group participants guiding them how to take part in this process, highlighting the following points:

Dreamwork Process

Pair up with another partner. One person will be the dreamer, and the other will be the facilitator of the dream work.

1. The dreamer tells the dream, highlighting the characters/symbols in the dream.

2. The dreamer will identify two or three characters and, in turn, speak as if they are that character, taking a first-person position by using the words 'I' or 'Me' and speaking as if the dream was happening now, in the present.
   - The facilitator will ask questions (remembering to stay close to the dreamers process) to:
     - Help the dreamer reflect.
     - Help the dreamer focus on their feelings and bodily sensations.
     - Facilitate the dreamer to communicate between the characters.
     - Example of 2 symbols—a dragon and a tree in the dreamer's dream, 'What is the 'dragon' saying to the tree?'

Near the end of the exploration, a discussion needs to take place concerning any links or insights made by the dreamer.

- **Important Notes for the Facilitator:**

  Do not inform the dreamer what their dream means—the dreamer takes ownership of the meaning of their dream, and another person cannot possibly understand the dreamer's dream!

  Therefore, avoid crossing boundaries. Remember to stay close to the dreamer's frame of reference and avoid making your own interpretations. This point is important in creating safety for the dreamer to engage in the dream work.
- Repeat the same process but change positions so that both of you can have a chance at being the dreamer and the facilitator.
- At the end of the session, there will be a whole-group debrief, during which you will share your experience of participating in the dreamwork as the dreamer and the facilitator. In addition, there will be a final section on feedback.

Working with Nightmares

Everyone will have occasional nightmares (Hartmann, 1984) particularly when experiencing stress, yet a minority of people can report regular nightmares. Nightmares can be defined "as very disturbing dreams, the events or emotions of which cause the dreamer to wake up". (Blagrove et al., 2004).

Cushway and Sewell (1992) suggested how most nightmares are associated with feeling helpless from some threat. For example, a threat can involve fear of loss such as losing a loved one through death or a relationship break down.

One strategy of working with a client who is experiencing distressing and frightening nightmares is to take a "story-line alteration" (Cushway & Sewell, 1992 p. 79) approach.

Following this method I have adapted this method to a pluralistic strategy which can have the effect of minimising the level of fear experienced by the client. An important point made by Cushway and Sewell (1992) is that they advise how the story-line alteration method is not appropriate for post-traumatic nightmares, associated with trauma which happened in waking life and trauma therapy would be more suitable in this case.

Pluralistic Strategy for Working with Nightmares

The therapist will offer this way of working to the client, suggesting how this strategy can reduce their feeling of fear. I would suggest they also inform the client that during this strategy there will be some repetition in telling the dream but this is an important part of the process.

Steps required to change the ending of the nightmare:

1. The therapist asks the client to tell the dream as if watching it as an observer.
2. Ask the client to tell the dream again using the words 'I' or 'Me' as if it is happening in the moment.

3. A two-way discussion follows regarding any links made by the client. Here, the therapist will ask dialogical questions, staying close to the client's communication to help them reflect deeper.
4. Ask the client how they could change the ending of the nightmare so it becomes less threatening. If the client is unsure, the therapist can offer a possible, less threatening ending. However, this suggestion needs to be acceptable to the client.
5. Suggest the client tell the dream again with this altered, less frightening ending.
6. Invite the client to work with this altered dream each night before sleep. If the client agrees to this, it is helpful to ask them if they can make a determined intention to practice speaking this dream with the altered ending out loud just before sleep.
7. Progress—In accordance with the pluralistic approach, feedback is highly valued. Therefore, checking in with the client on their progress in adopting this strategy each night and the impact it is having is essential, and this will be done in session in the coming weeks.

In summary, dreamwork has been of interest to various disciplines, including psychiatry, psychology, psychotherapy and counselling. Although various theoretical stances offer their particular understanding of dreams based on their underpinning theoretical stances, establishing methods for their clinical work, I adopt a pluralistic approach to working with a client's dreams.

The type of dreams a client might bring to therapy includes lucid dreams, dreams on loss, and nightmares. Two methods highlighted in this chapter have incorporated pluralistic adaptations from the Gestalt approach and the story-line alteration strategy.

References

Baird, B., Mota-Rolm, S. A., & Dresler, M. (2019). The cognitive neuroscience of lucid dreaming. *Neuroscience and Biobehavioral Reviews, 100*,

305–323. www.elsevier.com/locate/neuviorev, https://doi.org/10.1016/j.neubiorev.2019.03.008
Blagrove, M., Farmer, L., & Williams, E. (2004). The relationship of nightmare frequency and nightmare distress to well-being. *Journal of Sleep Research, 13*(2), 129–136. https://doi.org/10.1111/j.1365-2869.2004.00394.x
Bulkeley, K. (1995). *Spiritual dreaming: A cross-cultural and historical journey*. Paulist Press.
Cushway, D., & Sewell, R. (1992). *Counselling with dreams and nightmares. Counselling in practice*. Sage Publications.
Dresler, M., Kock, S. P., Spoomaker, V. I., Holsboer, F., Steiger, A., Samann, P. G., Obrig, H., & Czixch, M. (2011). Dreamed movement elicits activation in the sensorimotor cortex. *Current Biology, 21*, 1833–1837.
Freud, S. (1900). "The Interpretation of Dreams" released 1900. *A Science Odyssey: People and Discoveries*. PBS. 1998. Retrieved May 30, 2025.
Freud, S. (1910). The origin and development of psychoanalysis. *The American Journal of Psychology, 21*(2), 181–218. University of Illinois Press. https://www.jstor.org/stable/1413001
Freud, S. (1922, 1953). Dreams and telepathy. In G. Devereux (Ed.),*Psychoanalysis and the occult*. International Universities Press.
Gegenfurtner, N. (2005). *Eine empirische Studie über die gestalt-Klienten- und Therapeutenverhalten im Rahmen von 30 Ther-apiestunden*. Ludwig-Maximilians-Universität.
Harthan, J. (2013). *Working with dreams: A handbook of dream analysis techniques for individuals, therapists and dream groups*. Self published.
Hartmann, E. (1984). *The nightmare*. Basic Books.
Holzinger, B., Nierwetberg, F., Cosentino, L., & Mayer, L. (2021). Dream-SenseMemory—A gestalt-based dream-work approach embracing all our senses. *Research in Psychotherapy: Psychopathology, Process and Outcomes, 24*(529), 122–129.
Horton, C. L. (2020). Key concepts in dream research: cognition and consciousness are inherently linked but do no not control "Control"! *Frontiers in Human Neuroscience, 14*, Article 529, 1–4. https://doi.org/10.3389/frihum.2020.00259. www.frontiersin.org
Ichikawa, J. (2009). Dreams and Imagination. *Mind & Language: 24*(1), 103-121.
Jung, C. G. (1959). *Collected works of C. G. Jung, Volume 9: The archetypes and the collective unconscious* (2nd ed.). Princeton UP.
Jung, C. (1965). *Memories, dreams, reflections*. Vantage Books.
Jung, C. (1974). *Dreams* (Trans. R. F. C., Hull). Princeton University Press.

Jung, C. (1984). *Dream analysis: Notes of the seminar given in* 1928–30. Bollingen Series, Vol.99. University Press.
Jung, C. G. (1961). *Memories, dreams, reflections.* Recorded and edited by Aniela Jaffe. Pantheon Books.
Kubler-Ross, E. (1975). *Death, the final stage of growth.* Prentice Hall.
LaBerge, S. P., Nagel, L. E., Dement, W. C., & Zarcone jr, V. P., (1981). Lucid dreaming verified by volitional communication during REM sleep. *Perceptual Motor Skills, 52*(3), 727–732. National library of medicine. PubMed. https://doi.org/10.2466/pms.1981.52.3.727
LaBerge, S. P. (2015). Lucid dreaming: Metaconscience during paradoxical sleep. In M. K. M. Gluckman (Ed.), *Dream research: Contributions to clinical practice* (pp. 198–214). Routledge.
LoConto, D. G. (1998). Death & dreams: A sociological approach to grieving and identity. *Omega, 37*, 171–185.
Mallon, B. (2026). Dreams and bereavement. *Bereavement Care: 24*(3), 43-46.
McLeod, J. (2018). *Pluralistic therapy. Distinctive features*. Routledge. Taylor & Francis Group.
McGinn, C. (2004). *Mindsight: Image, dream meaning*. Cambridge, MA & London: Harvard University Press.
Metzger, W. (1936). *Gesetze des sehens* (4th ed.). Klotz.
Papayianni, F., & Cooper, M. (2017). Metatherapeutic communication: An exploratory analysis of therapist-reported moments of dialogue regarding the nature of the therapeutic work. *British Journal of Guidance & Counselling, 46*(1), 1–12. https://doi.org/10.1080/03069885.2017.1305098
Perls, F. (1970). Four lectures. In J. Fagan & I. Shepherd (Eds.), *Gestalt therapy now*. Science and Behavior Books, 27.
Perls, L. (1992). Concepts and misconceptions of Gestalt therapy. *Journal of Humanistic Psychology, 32*(3), 50–56. https://doi.org/10.1177/002216789 2323004
Perls, F. S., Hefferline, R. F., Goodman, P., & Perls, F. S. (1995). *Gestalttherapie: Grundlagen* (3. Aufl). Dt. Taschen-buchverl.
Ruby, P. M. (2011). Experimental research on dreams: state of the art and neuropsychoanalytical perspectives. *Frontiers in Psychology, 2*, 286. https://doi.org/10.3389/fpsyg2011.00286
Solms, M. (2000). Dreaming and REM sleep are controlled by different brain mechanisms. *Behaviour, Brain Science, 23*, 843–850. https://doi.org/ 10.1017/50140525X00003988
Van De Castle, R. L. (1994). *Our dreaming mind. A sweeping exploration of the role that dreams have played in politics, art, religion, and psychology, from*

ancient civilizations to the present day. Ballantine Books. ISBN 0-345-36435-X.

Van Eeden, F. (1913). A study of dreams. *Proceedings of the society for psychical research* (pp. 431–441).

Walker, M. P. (2009). REM, dreams and emotional brain homeostasis. *Frontiers Neuroscience, 3*, 442–443. https://walkerlab.berkeley.edu/reprints/Walker-REM-Emotion-FiN-2010-pdf

Windt, J. M. (2015). *Dreaming: A conceptual framework for philosophy of mind and empirical research.* MIT Press.

Wright, S. T., Kerr, C. W., Doroszcuk, N. M., Hang, P. C., & Luczkiewicz, D. L. (2014). *American Journal of Palliative Care, 31*(2), 132–138. https://doi.org/10.1177/1049909113479201

8

Drawing and Painting

Dewey et al. (1998) stated that art such as drawing and painting "is not the possession of the few recognized writers, painters, musicians, it is the authentic expression of any and all individuality" (p. 226). Bai Liu and Xin Li (2022) suggested that "the emergence of painting art therapy is a major breakthrough in humanistic medicine" (p. 24), with it being beneficial in clinical settings. The authors specify how engaging in visual art therapy, such as painting and drawing, using tools such as pencils, watercolours and oil paint enables the individual to move into the present moment in a mindfulness way, facilitating nonverbal processes, symbolism, and free expression that can aid reconstruction (Bail Liu & Xin Li, 2022). Mugisha (2024) argued how art-therapy "increases a person's understanding of their inner life and improves their overall health and well being" (p. 37).

An important factor when a client engages in artwork is for the therapist to be non-judgemental, staying alongside the client in their process. The aim is not the aesthetics of the image produced but to facilitate the client in creating a piece of work that represents their perceptions, emotions, and bodily sensations, which contribute to the integration of

D. Fleet, *Creative Interventions in Counselling and Psychotherapy*, Palgrave Texts in Counselling and Psychotherapy, https://doi.org/10.1007/978-3-032-16609-8_8

self (Sutarjo, 2023). Psychological and emotional healing are the ultimate goals. It is also helpful if the therapist avoids giving an opinion on the image drawn by the client, even if it is beautiful. If the client communicates that they are proud of what they have produced, the therapist can respond, affirming the client's opinion. However, it is necessary to stay in contact with the client's process. Giving compliments that emerge from the therapist's frame of reference can create expectations and indicate assessment, which can be unhelpful especially regarding the power balance in the relationship. The main message communicated to the client is that the meaning of the image and what it represents is the most important thing, rather than any artistic ability.

The British Association of Art Therapists (2022) described how art therapy can help clients to improve cognitive functioning, increase self-awareness and reduce inner conflict and distress. Runco (2014) was specific about how creative thinking can help individuals shift perspective, break routines, and facilitate original ideas to solve problems. Rubin (1986) conducted research on patients experiencing mental health disorders who engaged in art therapy and also stated that their artwork was related to inner conflict.

May (1994) agreed with the constructive outcome of art therapy and indicated how creative thinking is linked to psychological health. Malchiodi (1998) argued that visual arts help clients explore their inner experiences, Naumberg (1974) suggested how this symbolic form of expression involves therapists and clients interpreting unconscious experience and Damasio (2017) described how the whole mind is constructed of images.

When a therapist helps a client illustrate some of those symbolic images produced by drawing or painting it can foster deep reflection aiding personal growth, increase self-awareness and express emotional and psychological distress through self-expression. Unresolved issues are often associated with unexpressed emotions, and Malchiodi (1998) argued that therapeutic artwork aids a client in cathartic expression of unresolved pain. Cathartic expression involves acknowledging pent-up emotions that have been avoided or suppressed. Once the person can move beyond the emotional blockage, such expression can lead to immense relief. Bukar et al. (2019) state how catharsis has two components "the emotional aspect (strong emotional expression and processing) and the cognitive aspect of catharsis (insight, new realisation), and the unconscious becoming conscious" bringing positive change (p. 31).

Furthermore, Carson and Becker (2004) not only view working creatively as aiding "corrective emotional experiences" (p. 113) but also suggest that creativity can transform how a client and therapist relate to each other, which involves them experiencing things differently via their senses and intuition. As the client shares their inner discovery of their symbolic representations with an empathic therapist, the trust is deepened and for the client, a journey of self-compassion and self-acceptance can begin. Relief is experienced as previously repressed experiences are expressed both verbally and emotionally.

Several research studies have identified constructive change in clients' who have engaged in artwork in therapy (Edwards, 2004; Holmquist et al., 2017; Klimovsky et al., 1994; Maujean et al., 2014; Montag et al., 2014). Holmquist et al. (2017) researched clients' inner change during art therapy. They concluded that there was an increase in trust towards the therapist, an increase in emotional awareness, the development of conscious awareness, and an increase in ego strength. For example, a client may demonstrate an increase in their capacity to cope as they develop resilience and self-efficacy after coming to terms with a challenging experience. Maujean et al. (2014) were in agreement how clients engaging in art therapy can overcome difficulties and challenges in their lives. Carson and Becker (2004) suggested that a client who adopts drawing or painting in therapy can help them in communicating their sensory experience to the therapist, which contributes to corrective emotional experience.

Case Study: Laurence Using Drawing

When Laurence came to therapy his goal was for him to be able to let go of his past and focus on his future. In his past he shared how he had been neglected and experienced emotional and physical abuse. He had tried therapy before and although he said it had helped a little, he still felt there was work to be done. As his therapist, it was obvious that Laurence had the desire to move forward with his life and he was tired of his past continuing to have a huge hold on him. I asked him whether he had ever tried to work creatively and his response was,

> "No…but I will try it…I'll try anything".

We had a two-way discussion of the different methods of working creatively and he felt comfortable using pen and paper. We also had a discussion on whether he had done any Inner-Child work and he shared, he had tried it but wasn't very comfortable with it. I did share that it can be an uncomfortable process and that we could go at his pace and stop if he felt it was not working for him. He then shared,

> "maybe I wasn't ready to go there before".

I reached for the drawing pad and coloured pens, placed them on a small table in front of him and said,

> Therapist: "So when you think back to you as that little boy, neglected, can you form an image of him in your mind?'
> Laurence: "about 6 years old".
> T: Can you draw him…the image doesn't have to be perfect, the quality of the image doesn't matter…we are after the essence of that little boy…his thoughts and feelings.

Laurence sat for a little while then picked up a black biro (ignoring the coloured pens) and began to draw. He drew a tiny figure of a small boy in the corner of the page, surrounded by a box. Then he put the pen down and set his eyes on the image. I gave him space to begin talking when he was ready.

> L: That is me as a kid…trapped.

This was a powerful session with him sharing how insignificant he felt as a boy, nobody to really care for him. Laurence went on to share his painful experiences as a child. In the following therapy sessions, we both worked together on helping him give voice to the little boy within, that part which had gone into hiding and he came to realise that like in his past, nobody else could save him,

> "I have to save myself"

Over the weeks, Laurence had acknowledged the hurt he felt inside and expressed that. Sometimes it was an expression of fear, sometimes anger and at other times sadness. He began to feel a sense of relief and self-compassion and near the end of therapy, in his words:

> "I didn't get the right parents…they had their own troubles. I know it wasn't my fault, they just weren't good enough. But now I can put this down…don't need to carry this with me forever..time to move forward"

Some of my dialogical questions asked by me to help Laurence reflect and connect in a deep way to that 'Inner boy' were:

- If that little boy, trapped in the box, had a voice, what might he say to you now as the adult??
- What would you want to say to him in response?

However, I would advise that the therapist gently time their input and not speak over an active silence when it is apparent that the client is processing without speaking. If they closely observe the nonverbal behaviour of the client there is usually a good indication when the time is right for the therapist to offer a question or comment.

The image that Laurence drew was tiny, simple and colourless yet it had so much meaning and potential for him to explore his unresolved pain. I believe that this is a good example of the power of drawing in therapy that is not about the beauty or complexity of a drawing. It is the symbolic nature of the work itself that can help a client go deep into their inner-experience, helping to access that unresolved, repressed experience for processing, trying to understand and interpret the symbol in a safe way. Olga Rosa dos Remédios Rodrigues Souto (2024) argued how interpretation of the drawing or painting shows the hidden quality and helps to free the meaning of the symbols (p. 26867).

In addition, Milia (2000) highlights the self-soothing function of artwork in therapy and this element may be connected to the externalising process, the client is projecting their painful experience onto the paper, providing a 'protective distance" (Edgar-Bailey & Kress, 2010) as they engage in the art process.

With regard to a therapist's work with clients, Mooli Lahad (2000) employs expressive arts therapy in clinical supervision with his supervisees, including role-playing, drawing, imaginary dialogues, and the use of colours and shapes. His humanistic, creative supervision brings a fresh perspective to supervisees, helping them rethink their practice with clients.

BACP (2018) stated how "supervision is essential to how practitioners sustain good practice throughout their entire working life and good supervision is much more than case management. It includes working at depth" (p. 22). Furthermore, Milne (2007) views clinical supervision as an interpersonal process that involves supporting, directing and guiding therapists in their work with clients. Carroll (2007) expands on Milne's stance and suggests how experiential learning and reflection are also important features of supervision.

I am in agreement with Milne (2007) and Carroll (2007), but also support Lahad's approach (2000) that working creatively in supervision can bring a fresh perspective to a therapist, helping them gain insight into the therapeutic process, such as when they perceive a client as being blocked in their progress.

Case Study Using Drawing in Clinical Supervision—Steph

I was supervising Steph who was an experienced counsellor and clinical supervisor and had a tendency for self-criticism (Fleet, 2015a, 2015b). In one supervision session, I invited Steph to illustrate her 'Internal Supervisor', which she was happy to do (Image 8.1).

Patrick Casement (1985, 1990) coined the term 'Internal Supervisor', and when working constructively, the therapist has the ability to self-monitor, reflect and learn from their work with clients. Bell et al. (2016a, 2016b) suggested how developing a compassionate Internal Supervisor

Image 8.1 Steph's drawing of her Internal Supervisor

can be essential for the therapist. During supportive supervision, the supervisee can internalise aspects of the supervision (Casement, 1990) to develop an Internal Supervisor who is compassionate and also has the capacity to learn by reflecting on their practice, resulting in self-support and self-review. Bell et al., (2016a, 2016b) support Casement's view and argue how a self-compassionate Internal supervisor can "reduce worry, rumination and self-criticism whilst increasing self reflection" (p. 1), freeing the therapist to be more flexible in their work with clients.

However, issues such as self-criticism can hinder the development of a compassionate Internal Supervisor, and it is helpful for the supervisor to aid the supervisee in exploring such blocks to developing self-compassion.

Steph's image of her internal supervisor showed a face with staring eyes, frown lines, and a harsh, straight mouth, giving the impression of a grimace. She labelled it "The Bitch".

I asked Steph,

'What sort of messages do you feel come from The Bitch?'

Steph replied,

"You're rubbish! You're so crap! Call yourself a counsellor!"

I responded to Steph, saying,

"Those messages are so critical and judgemental of your work….and you wouldn't say that to one of your supervisees"

Steph responded,

"Oh God No!".

(Fleet, 2015a, 2015b, pp. 16–17)

These internal critical messages were having a negative impact on Steph, resulting in her feeling de-skilled at this time and her taking responsibility for a client who she described as being stuck in the therapeutic process.

Further on in the session, I asked Steph how the image would look if it were less threatening, and she began to alter the image using a red and blue pen. She altered the mouth to make it less harsh, adding a smile, then coloured in the eyes to give a softer expression and added a heart in red ink. As Steph observed the altered image, she began to re-script the messages, which resulted in a healthier revision that encouraged reflexivity.

In speech bubbles she wrote,

"Not sure that worked"
"Try something different"
"What was behind that?"
(Fleet, 2015a, 2015b, pp. 16–17).

Steph renamed her Internal Supervisor as 'My Line Manager', which seemed to bring a different perspective for her. She began to take a more self-compassionate stance when reflecting on her work with her client. This change in her perspective seemed to free her up to find different ways of working with her client to help them engage in the therapeutic process.

Early and Weiss (2013) suggest in their work with the inner critic that a person can become the victim of negative messages about their self-worth. They identify a range of inner critics, one of which is 'The Underminer', which seems to apply to Steph. After working creatively, Steph realised how such negative messages were blocking her from seeing her actual ability. Although I reassured Steph about her ability, she had to see this for herself.

As Steph's supervisor, this session served as a valuable reminder for me. I viewed Steph as a highly competent and caring therapist. However, any therapist can experience moments when their confidence is shaken, and it is essential that supervisors help the supervisee work through this issue.

Drawing and Painting Online

I offer one-to-one and group therapy online, utilising creative approaches, such as drawing and painting, to support my clients. In the initial session, the option of working creatively is explored, and a two-way dialogical conversation is important so we can establish the best way of working for that client and in the group context I offer various creative methods which clients can choose from.

Many of my clients are enthusiastic about trying creative work, and I have witnessed them experiencing real benefits from working this way. Such benefits have included the expression of unresolved emotions, personal insight into problems, an increase in self-esteem, and shifts in attitudes with them adopting a more positive frame of mind.

In my online practice, clients have engaged in drawing and painting in between sessions. For example, several clients have shared how they feel angry due to the way they were treated, either during their childhood, teenage years, or as adults. Issues have ranged from abuse, bullying, neglect and abandonment. Once the client has expressed a desire to work creatively, I offer suggestions for illustrating their anger (or experiences of abuse, bullying, neglect, or abandonment) by drawing a symbol on paper to represent the emotion they are currently experiencing that is difficult to manage. I then suggest they focus on the completed drawing or painting and engage in free writing. This free writing will involve writing down any thoughts or feelings that arise from observing their image. The client will then bring their reflections (and usually the image they have produced) to the next therapy session for further exploration.

In addition to working with individual clients, structured drawing and painting are routinely used in group therapy and are viewed as a method that can contribute to therapeutic change (Stone & Everts, 2006) and aid in deep emotional expression (Fan et al., 2019). For example, therapists facilitating groups who are experiencing substance misuse often facilitate individuals within the group to draw or paint blocks representing their difficulty in abstaining from their addiction. This drawing or painting is then usually explored using the written word and/or shared with the group. Lorenz et al (2022) argued how sharing with the therapy group can have a positive impact on individual motivation to change substance use behaviour. McDonald (2023) suggested how expressive art therapy strategies, such as drawing and painting help to develop “coping mechanisms for substance use recovery” (p. 1).

Drawing and painting is commonly used in group counselling supervision. Shiflett and Remley (2014) argue how using this type of creative expression can yield positive outcomes for the group supervision process.

In the past, as a recently qualified therapist, I attended a group supervision session. Although this happened many years ago, I still have a clear memory of being asked to illustrate the block regarding my work with a client who was struggling to engage, with the therapeutic process seeming stuck. I found this exercise both powerful and enlightening, and drew an image of a brick wall. The group supervisor asked me to explore my feelings about this visual metaphor, what it looked like, how it felt as I imagined touching it and how I could get beyond that wall. This approach helped me shift my perspective as the cause of the block, from my client to me as the therapist. The outcome helped me to be more present with the client, but in a different way. In the next session,

I was able to be more congruent with the client, and we focused on what we were both finding difficult in our work together. This dialogical conversation resulted in both of us (client and therapist) being open, which helped to establish a greater connection, helping progression of the therapeutic process.

Regarding the use of drawing and painting in online therapy, my experience with clients has shown that they feel at ease in their own homes, and their willingness to engage with this strategy is usually positive. My experience is that when the client brings their artwork to the following session, this has a positive impact on building trust in the relationship. Choi et al. (2014) support this claim, stating that clients feel more comfortable engaging in therapy in their own homes. They also note the positive impact on clients who experience social isolation due to personal circumstances, such as geographical location or mobility difficulties. Keisari et al. (2022) are in agreement and state, "clients' home environment in the therapy provides an opportunity to develop deeper trust in the therapeutic relationship" (p. 3). However, for some clients the home environment is not conducive for then to engage in such strategies and the therapy room might be the only place they feel safe to share their experience.

Some clients welcome the convenience of accessing therapy via a computer or smartphone. Once the session is over, the client is already home without having to make the journey back. Furthermore, travelling to a different location, sitting in a waiting room, being seen by others, and then having to travel home once the session is complete can put some clients off when seeking therapy. Additionally, some clients appreciate the greater level of anonymity, with only the therapist being aware of their identity during therapy.

In summary, art therapy, which utilises drawing and painting, can alleviate emotional and psychological distress by facilitating inner discovery and self-expression of unresolved issues, bringing about constructive change for the client. Furthermore, this creative method can be applied in various clinical contexts, including face-to-face therapy, online therapy, group therapy, and individual and group clinical supervision.

References

Bell, T., Dixon, A., & Kolts, R. (2016). Developing a compassionate internal supervisor: compassion-focussed therapy for trainee therapists. *Clinical Psychology and Psychotherapy.* Published online: John Wiley & Sons, Ltd. wileyonlinelibrary.com, https://doi.org/10.1002/cpp.2031. Retrieved 1 July, 2025.

British Association for Counselling and Psychotherapy. (2018). *Ethical Framework for the counselling professions.* Lutterworth. www.bacp.co.uk

Bai, Liu, & Xin, Li. (2022). *Breakthrough in humanistic medicine: Research on the rise and principle of painting art therapy.* 5th International Conference on Modern Approach in Humanities and Social Sciences. ICMHS. 08–10 July, 2022. Zurich, Switzerland. www.icmhs.org, Retrieved June 20, 2025.

Bell, T., Dixon, A., & Kolts, R. (2016). Developing a compassionate internal supervisor: Compassion-focused therapy for trainee therapists. *Clinical Psychology and Psychotherapy*. Copyright © 2016 John Wiley & Sons, Ltd. Published online in Wiley Online Library (wileyonlinelibrary.com). https://doi.org/10.1002/cpp.2031, Retrieved June 26, 2025.

British Association of Art Therapists (BAAT). (2022). *What is art therapy?* [online]. https://www.baat.org/About-Art-Therapy [Accessed April 23, 2022].

Bukar, A., Abdullah, A., Opara, J. A., Abdulkadir, M., & Hassan, A. (2019). Catharsis as a therapy: An overview on health and human development. *Journal of Physical Health and Sports Medicine, 2*, 31–35. https://doi.org/10.36811/jphsm.2019.110007

Carroll, M. (2007). One more time: What is supervision? *Psychotherapy in Australia, 13*, 34–37.

Carson, D. K., & Becker, K. W. (2004). When lightening strikes: Reexamining creativity in psychotherapy. *Journal of Counseling & Development, 82*, 111–115. https://doi.org/10.1002/j.1556-6678.2004.tb00292.x

Casement, P. (1985). *On learning from the patient*. Tavistock.

Casement, P. (1990). *Further learning from the patient: The analytic space and process*. Tavistock.

Choi, N. G., Hegel, M. T., Marti, C. N., Marinucci, M. L., Sirrianni, L., & Bruce, M. (2014). Telehealth problem-solving therapy for depressed low-income homebound older adults. *American Journal of Geriatric Psychiatry, 22*, 263–276.

Dewey, J., Hickman, L., & Alexander. T. (1998). *The essential dewey: Pragmatism, education, democracy* (Vol. 1). Indiana University Press.

Damasio, A. (2017). A Estranha Ordem das Coisas. *A Vida, os SenT.mentos e as Culturas* (pp. 132–133). Temas e Debates.

Earley, J., & Weiss, B. (2013). *Freedom from your inner critic: A self-therapy approach*. Sounds True.

Edgar-Bailey, M., & Kress, V. E. (2010). Resolving child and adolescent traumatic grief: Creative techniques and interventions. *Journal of Creativity in Mental Health, 5*, 158–176. https://doi.org/10.1080/15401383.2010.507657

Edwards, D. (2004). *Art therapy*. SAGE.

Fleet, D. (2015). Ways of Working. Beyond words: Creative methods have an established evidence-base when working with children and young people but why are they not more widely used when counselling adults? *Private Practice*, Spring 2015 (pp. 15–17). British Association for Counselling and Psychotherapy. https://www.bacp.co.uk

Fan, L., Chun, Y., & Yuanchun, S. (2019). Guided social sharing of emotions through drawing art therapy: generation of deep emotional expression and helpful emotional responses. Chinese CH1'19: *Proceedings of the Seventh International Symposium of Chinese CH1*. pages 65078 https://doi.org/10.1145/3332169.3333571, retrieved 5 July, 2025.

Fleet, D. (2015). Ways of working beyond words: Creative methods have an established evidence-base when working with children and young people but why are they not more widely used when counselling adults? *Private Practice*, Spring 2015 (pp. 15–17). British Association for Counselling and Psychotherapy. https://www.bacp.co.uk

Holmquist, G., Roxberg, A., Larsson, I., & Lundqvist-Persson, C. (2017). What art therapists consider to be patients' inner-change and how it may appear during art therapy. *The Arts in Psychotherapy, 56*(45–52). https://doi.org/10.1016/j.aip.2017.07.005

Keisari, S., Piol, S., Elkarif, T., Mota, G., & Testoni, I. (2022). Crafting life stories in photocollege: An online creative art-based intervention for older adults. *Behavioral Science, 12*(1), 1–23.

Klimovsky, G., Vainer, S. B., de Goldenberg, D. B., de Kuitca, M. K., de Liberman, J. F., & Siniavsky, M. (1994). Change in psychoanalysis: Epistemological aspects. *International Journal of Psychoanalysis, 75*(Pt 1.), 51–58.

Lahad, M. (2000). *Creative Supervision: The use of expensive arts methods in supervision and self-supervision, England*. Jessica Kingsley Publishers Ltd.

Lorenz, H., Stuebing, M. D., Nambeye, C., Lungo, G., & Littlefield, L. M. (2022). Substance use treatment using cultural arts and 12 steps: Curriculum training and community-led implementation in Zambia. *Addictive Behaviors Reports, 15*(100424–). https://doi-org.ezproxyles.flo.org/10.1016/j.abrep.2022.100424
Malchiodi, C. (1998). *The art therapy sourcebook*. Lowell House.
May, R. (1994). *The courage to create*. Norton.
Maujean, A., Peppeing, C., & Kendall, E. (2014). A systemic review of randomized controlled studies in art therapy. *Art Therapy, 3*(1), 37–44. https://doi.org/10.1080/07421656.2014.873696
McDonald, Z. (2023). Using expressive arts therapy to develop coping mechanisms to manage substance use. *Expressive Therapies Capstone Theses, 661*, Spring, 5(21). https://digitalcommons.lesley.edu/expressive_theses/66/ retrieved 6 July, 2025.
Milia, D. (2000). *Self-mutilation and art therapy: Violent creation.* Jessica Kingsley.
Milne, D. (2007). An empirical definition of clinical supervision. *British Journal of Clinical Psychology, 46*, 437–447. https://doi.org/10.1348/014466507X197415
Montag, C., Haase, L, Seidel, D., Bayerl, M., Gallin at, J., & Hermann, U. et.al. (2014). A pilot RCT of psychoanalysis group art therapy for patients in acute psychotic episodes. Feasibility impact on symptoms and mentalising capacity. *Public Library of Science, 9*(11), e112348. https://doi.org/10.1371/journal.pone,0112348
Mugisha, E. K. (2024). The therapeutic effects of art therapy in mental health. *Eurasian Experiment Journal of Scientific and Applied Research, 5*(3), 37–40.
Naumberg, M. (1974). *An introduction to art therapy: Studies of the "free' art expression of behavior problem Children and Adolescents as a means of diagnosis and therapy*. Teachers College Press ISBN-13978-080772425.5
Olga Rosa dos Remédios Rodrigues Souto. (2024). The importance of psychotherapy developed through the color of drawing and painting. *International Journal of Current Research, 16*(01), 26867–26869.
Rubin, J. A. (1986). From psychopathology to psychotherapy through art expression: A focus on Hans Prinzhorn and others. *Art Therapy, 3*(1), 27–33.
Runco, M. A. (2014). *Creativity: Theories and themes: Research, development and practice* (2nd ed.). Elsevier.
Shiflett, C. L., & Remley, JR, T. (2014). Incorporating case conceptualization drawing in counselor group supervision: A grounded theory study. *Journal*

of Creativity in Mental Health, 9(1), 33–52. https://doi.org/10.1080/15401383.2013.878680

Stone, C., & Everts, H. (2006). The therapeutic use of metaphor in interactive drawing therapy. *New Zealand Journal of Counselling,26*(4), 31–43. https://doi.org/10.24135/nzjc.v2614.65

Sutarjo, J. (2023). Painting as a means of art therapy for children-children with autism spectrum disorder (Case study in Kaliwungu Kudus State Extraordinary School). *Jurnal Indonesia Social Sains, 4*(02), 97–105.

9

Breathing Techniques, Working with the Five Senses and the Use of Touch

Breathing Techniques

Within the broad field of mental health, breathing techniques for stress and anxiety are widely used. Individuals who experience anxiety often worry about particular things, causing them distress. Pothis et al. (2024) describe how people with generalised anxiety disorder (GAD) "are excessively anxious about everyday concerns…and some symptoms…include worry, restlessness, insomnia, exhaustion, irritability, sweating and shaking" (p. 612). Whether the individual is suffering from anxiety or excessive anxiety, breathing strategies may help to ease the intensity of their stress and foster a calmer mind to help decrease the associated symptoms. Furthermore, the process of breathing is arguably the only part of our autonomic nervous system that automatically controls bodily functions, in which we can consciously take back control and therefore choose to affect our somatic and psychological state. In addition, Betka et al. (2022) stated how "Breathing control can be automatic or voluntary and is thus related to consciousness" (https://doi.org/https://doi.org/10.1016/j.biopsycho.2022.108329 retrieved 3 September 2025.

Steinmane and Fernate (2025) agree that breathing exercises can have a positive impact on mental well-being by promoting relaxation,

D. Fleet, *Creative Interventions in Counselling and Psychotherapy*, Palgrave Texts in Counselling and Psychotherapy, https://doi.org/10.1007/978-3-032-16609-8_9

reducing stress, and enhancing sleep quality. Furthermore, Tsai et al. (1995) suggest how breathing strategies can significantly improve the quality of life, giving short-term and long-term relief.

Cortes-Vazquez. (2024) suggested how breathing strategies can be divided into two basic categories of "breath awareness and breath control" (p. 1). Breath awareness or mindful breathing involves focusing attention on the breath but without trying to control it (Pozuelos et al., 2019).

The most studied breathing intervention for physical and mental health is slow breathing (Fincham et al., 2023). Breathing control concerns the act of consciously altering the frequency of the breath, depth of the breath, the frequency of inhalation and exhalation, and movement of the breath from where it is situated in the body, including the stomach, chest, nose, or mouth (Fincham et al., 2023). Paced slow breathing aims to reduce the breath rate and usually involves between ten (Zaccaro et al., 2018) or six breaths (Laborde et al., 2017) per minute.

As I adopt a pluralistic approach and value collaboration between client and therapist, I believe it is essential to invite the client into the decision-making process concerning the choice of strategy. Then if the client wants to try out the paced slow breathing strategy, this can be done first by the therapist guiding the client through this exercise in the session. The therapist could offer that the client tries out the six and the ten breaths per minute to see which suits them best.

However, there are a wide range of breathing strategies that fit into one of these two categories, adopted by different health professionals in their work with clients. Bentley et al. (2023) state how "Anxiety and stress plague populations worldwide" (p. 1) and suggest how breathing techniques can be effective in addressing this epidemic. Although Bentley et al.'s (2023) systematic review suggested that breathing strategies can be effective in decreasing stress, effectiveness will be influenced by the type of breathing strategy, how it is implemented, and the individual engaging with the breathing strategy. These researchers identified factors to increase the effectiveness of breathing techniques including:

- The pace of breathing and to have some regulated slow breathing in the strategy.

- For the client to follow a human voice as a guide to practicing the strategy, especially when new to this type of practice.
- To consider the set up prior to the breathing strategy, such as finding a quiet space and sitting or laying down in a comfortable position.
- Length of practice—with each exercise lasting at least five minutes and for the client to practice this breathing strategy regularly.

Adapted from Bentley et al. (2023, p. 31)

The factors proposed by Bentley et al. (2023) and adapted could be communicated to the client either verbally or giving written prompts to help them remember when practising in between therapy sessions.

Other Types of Breathing Strategies

Box Breathing—A Breath Control Strategy

The United States Navy SEALS use the four-step box breathing strategy when in high-stress circumstances, believed to aid the management of stress and overall health.

(https://www.medicinenet.com/why_do_navy_seals_use_box_breathing/article.htm retrieved 1 August 2025). Ahmed et al (2022) described how box breathing is a slow breathing method, also known as square breathing, which is a powerful stress relief strategy and also helps with the level of concentration. Balban et al. (2023) support Ahmed et al.'s stance, suggesting how box breathing helps to manage stress and cultivates a calm mind.

- An example of box breathing:

  1. Find a quiet space and sit with your back straight.
  2. Breathe in through the nose counting for 4 seconds.
  3. Then hold the breath for a count of 4
  4. Breathe out through the mouth for a count of 4

5. Hold the breath for a count of 4
6. Repeat the exercise 5 times

Adapted from Wei. (2023) psyhologytoday.com/gb/blog/urban-survival202303/try-box-breathing-to-reduce-anxiety-and-stress retrieved 10 July, 2025.

When working with clients experiencing a range of overwhelming emotions, by taking a pluralistic approach, I suggest a range of different breathing strategies so they can consider which would suit them best as a way of managing their distress in between sessions. Through dialogical conversation, it is helpful to explore which strategy they favour. The box breathing strategy has been helpful to several of my clients, but their individual preferences are important in that decision-making process. As their therapist, I will also regularly check in with them to receive their feedback on how helpful their chosen strategy is and whether anything needs to be adapted to make it as effective as possible.

4-7-8 Breathing

The 4-7-8 breathing strategy originates from ancient yogic practices, with Dr Weil an American physician, bringing notable attention for its potential when helping individuals who have difficulty when sleeping (Russo et al., 2017).

The strategy involves, breathing in through the nostrils for a count of 4, holding the breath for a count of 7 and breathing out through the mouth for a count of 8 (Vierra et al., 2022) and is now a popular coping exercise used across various psychological interventions. The benefit of this exercise is in its simplicity, which makes it easy to practice for individuals from all walks of life.

Mindful Breathing—A Breath Awareness Strategy

Komariah et al. (2023) argued how Mindfulness-based therapeutic approaches are currently gaining ground in popular therapy among the world community and mindful breathing is being adopted by therapists who see the value of this strategy with their clients who experience anxiety and other conditions associated with distress.

The mindful breathing approach, adopted by therapists, considers the connection between mind and body as a central feature to help a client avoid experiencing triggered stress responses (Benson et al., 2011: 1–9; Kabri & Surya, 2023).

Kabri and Surya (2023) suggested how the body registers stress before the conscious mind does and they indicate how the individual can learn to recognise this when it begins to happen through muscle tension. In mindfulness breathing the client is taught how to 'let go' of the breath and sensations and avoid clinging to different desires. This also involves letting go of resistance to everything that can reduce stress. Marotta (2013) identified this process as 'pressing the pause button" so the individual can minimise feelings of insecurity and increase awareness and connection with themself (pp. 23–72).

A mindful breathing guide to help a client engage in this exercise

- Speaking in a softly spoken voice and relaxed pace guide the client to sit in a comfortable chair/position.
- Invite them to close their eyes if they wish to.
- Encourage them to relax and drop their shoulders (you can usually see their posture change and their shoulders drop).
- Then guide them using the following prompts:
  - Focus on your breath.
  - Notice the sensations of inhaling and exhaling as the air enters and leaves your body.
  - Notice the rise and fall of your chest or stomach as you breathe.
  - Take a few deep breaths.
  - Now allow your breath to return to its natural rhythm.
  - Observe your thoughts and feelings without any judgement.
  - If your mind wanders, gently bring back your attention to your breath.
  - (When the practice is complete, gently guide them to become aware of their surroundings).

- Move your fingers and toes, your hands and feet and become aware of the chair beneath you.

After the session, invite the client to share how they feel after their practice and any thoughts they have on using this technique to manage their distress in between sessions.

Body Scan Breathing (A Mindfulness Strategy)

Kabat-Zinn (2002) described the definition of Body Scan Breathing concerns the process of paying attention to the present moment in a non-judgemental way, aiding the unfolding of experience moment by moment. When combined with awareness, acceptance and curiosity, this can alter the relationship with the content, causing distress. The aim here is to foster a sense of control and sensory awareness by being aware of bodily sensations, the breath, emotions and associated thoughts about the present moment. Furthermore, sights and sounds in the immediate external environment are also focused on (Colgan & Wahbeh, 2016).

Mehling et al. (2008) stated how the body scan enhances the felt sense that is localised within the body and suggest there is a difference between an individual thinking about the body and perceiving it and developing this awareness of perceiving the body in this way can help to manage psychological and emotional distress.

I can see how each of the above breathing exercises can be beneficial for different individuals who will have their preference in using a strategy to manage their anxiety and distress. Moreover, offering various methods to clients and involving them in the decision-making process will respect their autonomy and freedom of choice.

In my practice, I offer various breathing strategies to clients experiencing a range of issues. Breathing strategies can help with worry and anxiety, low mood and depression, overwhelming emotional distress, fear or anger. Furthermore, individual clients will have different attitudes and ways of processing, which will also impact the strategy they choose to practice. For example, a client who is more cognitive and tends to intellectualise might be more suitable for the box breathing strategy. However, a client who tends to be creative might feel more at ease using a creative visualisation and focusing on the breath. A different client who is in tune with their bodily sensations may be drawn to a breathing strategy that incorporates the body. Duros and Crowley (2014) argue that "in the recent past, traditional psychotherapy has concentrated on mind first, body second" (p. 237) and suggest that the tremendous rise in interest in neurobiology has created a shift with many professionals within the field of mental health now viewing the body as a vehicle for change.

I have found that when a breathing strategy is offered the combination of incorporating breathing, visualisation and focusing on the body usually gets the attention of most clients and once I take them through this strategy, they find it useful in managing their distress. Below is such a strategy I have constructed to offer to clients which incorporates colour for clients who view themselves as creative. However, the exercise can be used without using colour.

Breathing Visualisation for Anxiety (or Any Distressing Feeling)—Using Colour

Before beginning the breathing strategy below ask yourself the following two questions:

1. Scan your body and where do you feel the anxiety (pain, anger, etc.)?
   This could be in the chest area, the lower abdomen or anywhere. Once you have located where your anxiety sits in your body, tune into that anxiety and imagine a colour associated with it (possibly red, purple or any colour that comes to mind).
2. Now, when you imagine a calm state, what colour is associated with that?
   Could be light blue, yellow, green or any colour that comes to mind.

Now follow the breathing strategy below:

Sit comfortably and close your eyes. Focus your mind on your breathing, slowly and gently breath in through your nose, out through your mouth.....in and out...in and out....in and out.
Now move your attention to the top of your head, feel your scalp relax. Now relax the muscles in your face, like ice melting. Relax the muscles in your neck and shoulders and feel your shoulders drop. Relax the muscles in your back, feel them soften, just let go. Now relax the muscles in your chest...arms...hands...and fingers. Then the stomach area...just let go. Relax the muscles in your hip area...thighs...knees...feet...and toes.
Now scan your body to feel where the anxiety (feeling) sits, place your hands over this area. See and feel that anxiety...does a colour come to mind as you tune into your anxiety? (e.g. ***RED*** *but could be any colour).*
[If the client does not want to incorporate colour, the therapist can just refer to the distressing emotion]
Imagine and feel this ***RED*** *anxiety move up your body, up your throat and breathe this out through your mouth.*
*Now visualise a calm, healing energy - what colour is this? (e.g.****BLUE*** *but could be any colour) breathe in this calm* ***BLUE*** *energy gently through your nose, and see this* ***BLUE*** *energy moving to that place in your body where the anxiety sits...mixing with the anxiety. Repeat this as many times as you need to until you feel calmer and the anxiety dissipates.*

With time and practice you should be able to manage your anxiety more effectively.

A similar strategy can be used for a client experiencing physical pain.

Breathing Technique for Pain Management

Find a calm and relaxing place to sit or lay down where you won't be disturbed. Once you are settled, tune into your pain, wherever it is in your body. From 1–10 give it a number of how painful it is 1 = low pain with 10 = being severe pain.

- Visualise the pain and where it sits in your body. See and feel it moving up towards your mouth and begin to breathe it out at a slow pace.

- Then slowly breathe in a calm, healing energy, gently through your nose, and see and feel this moving to where the pain is located in your body.
- Continue this exercise until the pain begins to subside and you are breathing in calm, healing energy, and breathing out calm, healing energy.
- After the breathing has stopped, then give yourself a number on how the pain feels now.
- You can keep a record of this each day to monitor your progress.

This exercise takes practice, the more you try and relax and practice often the more effective it can become.

Five Senses Grounding Exercise

Bokarius (2020) states how "the senses play an important role in multiple domains of functioning, both physical and psychological" (p. 449). Furthermore, each sense can initiate emotions that may be pleasant or unpleasant and evoke memories that are linked to "anxiety, panic attacks, flashbacks, anger or depression" (p. 449).

Taking the significance of this core element of human nature into account, I value the role of incorporating the five senses in any therapeutic approach, which could be extremely helpful for the client's process. To avoid integrating this core element of humanity into therapy seems incomprehensible to me, and I believe the five senses can be as significant to a client's pain and distress as thinking and emotion are and deserve a place in any therapeutic approach.

I have discovered how working with clients who have severe and overwhelming anxiety or fear, that sometimes it is too difficult for the client to focus on a visualisation or on their breathing. The more simple strategy of focusing on their five senses when they are feeling overwhelmed can be extremely helpful to them.

The exercise below can be explained to the client in the therapy session and I often find that the client will write down the five questions to remind themselves, once they leave the session.

Five Senses Exercise for Overwhelming Distress

When feeling overwhelmed and out of control emotionally, ask yourself the following five questions:

Questions	Examples but could be anything
What do I **See?**—	Birds flying outside, chair, dog, houseplant.
What do I **Hear?**—	Wind outside, washing machine, people talking.
What do I **Smell?**—	Own perfume, cologne, food cooking.
What do I **Taste?**—	Coffee you just drank, meal you just ate.
What is **Touching me?**—	Chair beneath me, clothes against my skin.

I have found the following guidance to be helpful to clients:

This exercise brings you into the 'here and now', moving you away from worrying about what has happened in the past (recent or long ago) or what might happen. It can help with anxiety or being preoccupied with your fearful and negative thoughts, bringing you into the here and now.

The Benefits of Touch

Building on the question of touch as incorporated in the five senses exercise above, there is a need for greater recognition of how touch can be beneficial within counselling and psychotherapy. Within the literature, the primary focus is on touch between therapist and client. Some literature acknowledges how a gentle touch, such as a light touch on the hand, can be supportive, and some therapists view hugging a client who has agreed to this type of touch as establishing a trusting therapeutic relationship (Caldwell, 2002; Carere-Comes, 2007; Shaw, 2003; Zur & Nordmarken, 2004). However, there is a risk associated with boundary crossing, which may have a detrimental impact on the client (Zur, 2007).

Wolberg (1954) took a more extreme stance on the negative implications of touching a client and argued that touch within the therapeutic relationship is taboo, and argued against it, suggesting the client may misinterpret the meaning, with a risk of communicating a sexual connotation if a client is touched by their therapist. Furthermore, Rothschild (2002) warned how such touch can be invasive for a client who has experienced sexual abuse in childhood.

Taking the risks into consideration, if touch between therapist and client is to be a potential part of the professional relationship, then explicit permission of the client needs to be gained and respected each time so as to avoid any boundary break.

My own practice with clients has led me to the conclusion that the issue of touch has a broader application than only touch between therapist and client. In Chapter 6 of this text, touch was explored when using objects and sand trays, enabling the expression of unresolved emotion, and touch can be incorporated in other ways. For example, animal-assisted therapy (AAT) and hospital visits, where dogs are taken to meet patients, are becoming increasingly common. AAT is a contemporary form of help for people with anxiety and other distressing issues, which has multiple benefits (Brandao et al., 2025). The stroking and petting of dogs by patients helps to soothe and reduce stress levels in patients/clients (Pichot, 2012).

In my own practice, clients have often enquired about my friendly, well-trained pet dog, and once I offered them the chance to meet and stroke my pet, many have enthusiastically asked to. On many occasions, clients have stroked and petted my dog, which shifts them into a more relaxed state. I believe this has helped them feel at ease, so they can begin to settle before therapy begins. It also appears to have a positive contribution to building the therapeutic relationship. I have had clients who, at the end of the session, have asked to see my dog before leaving, which appears to bring an ease about ending the session. It is like they have moved out of the client position, bringing a grounding moment, helping them to get on with the rest of their day as they leave.

However, during the initial appointment, I found it essential to mention that the dog is friendly, aiming to put the client at ease. This communication also enables me to assess whether the client is frightened of dogs, and if so, I take action by ensuring the dog is not present in the house before the therapy begins.

Another current trend which incorporates the use of touch is the availability of therapy toys not only for children but also intended for adults who need comfort. The Sloth therapy bear is a product that has weighted legs to provide comfort and stress relief to mirror the act of having a hug. The act of cuddling the bear and feeling its weight around the neck and shoulders can initiate a calming experience, and I have observed a visible shift in body language indicating relaxation when a client has held this bear. These therapy bears can be utilised both inside and outside the therapy room by the client. An example of an adult client who was having trouble sleeping had recently changed her life and was now living alone. She decided to purchase the Sloth Bear, and in a later session, she was surprised by how this bear had provided comfort, helping her to drift off to sleep at night.

I believe that the use of touch in therapy can bring comfort and relief to some clients, and I think the benefits are largely underacknowledged. I have known therapists who work with adult clients who have experienced childhood sexual abuse, and the therapists placed soft toys such as teddy bears in their therapy room. Often, when a client is having difficulty speaking about the abuse they experienced, holding a soft toy, which they can stroke and sometimes hide behind when they have difficulty making eye contact with the therapist, can help them begin to speak the unspeakable that they have kept secret for so long.

In summary, various breathing strategies can be helpful for a therapist to offer a client as an exercise to practice managing their distress between therapy sessions. A pluralistic approach would involve engaging in a dialogical conversation, allowing the client to be involved in the decision-making process to determine the best strategy for them. Therefore, the therapist would need to be aware of a range of breathing strategies to offer to the client. In addition, if the client tends to become overwhelmed with their emotions, it might serve them better to use the five-senses exercise to help ground them and bring them back to the 'here and now', so they move their attention away from worrying about what may happen and what has happened to focus on the present moment. Further strategies that incorporate touch, which have several benefits, include gentle, appropriate therapist touch, provided there is explicit client permission, as well as incorporating strategies from animal-assisted therapy, soft toys and weighted therapy toys.

References

Ahmed, A. A., Devi, R. G., & Priya, A. J. (2022). Effect of box breathing technique on lung function test. *Journal of Pharmaceutical Research International, 33*(58A), 25–31, 2021; Article no.JPRI.78935 ISSN: 2456-9119 (Past name: British Journal of Pharmaceutical Research, Past ISSN: 2231-2919, NLM ID: 101631759)

Balben, M. Y., Neri, E., Kogon, M. M., Weed, L., Nouriani, B. J., Jo, B., Holl, G., Zeitzer, J. M., Spiegel, D., & Huberman, A. D. (2023). Brief structured respiration practices enhance mood and reduce physiological practices enhance mood and reduce physiological arousal. *Cell reports Medicine, 4*(1), 100895 https://doi.org/10.1016/j/cr2022.100895

Benson, H., Casey, A., Dadoly, A., Coltera, F., Allison, K. Cahill., Harvard Medical School., & Harvard Medical School. Health Publications Group. (2011: 1–9). *Stress management: Approaches for preventing and reducing stress.* Harvard Health Publications.

Bentley, T. G. K., Andrea-Penna, G., Rakie, M., Arce, N., LaFaille, M., Berman, R., Cooley, K., & Sprimont, P. (2023). Breathing practices for stress and anxiety reduction: Conceptual Framework of Implementation. Guidelines Based on a systematic review of the published literature. MDPI *Brain Science, 13*, 1612, 1–52.

Betka, S., Adler, D., Similowski, T., & Blanke, O. (2022). Breathing control, brain, and bodily self-consciousness: Toward immersive digiceuticals to alleviate respiratory suffering. *Biological Psychology, 171*, May 2022, 108329, 1–16. https://doi.org/10.1016/j.biopsycho.2022.108329

Bokarius, V. (2020). *Engaging in the five senses: taste, smell, see, listen, touch.* Chapter 37, pp. 448–462, The Handbook of Wellness Medicine. Editor: Waguih William Ishake. Cambridge, UK. Cambridge University Press.

Brandao, C., Sampaio, M., Sousa-Gomes, V., Favero, M., & Moreira, D. (2025, January 6). Effects of Animal-assisted therapy for anxiety reduction in children and adolescents: A systematic review. *Journal of Clinical Medicine, 14*(1), 287. https://doi.org/10/3390/jcm14010287

Caldwell, C. (2002, June). *Using touch in psychotherapy.* Paper presented at the USA Body Psychotherapy Conference, Baltimore.

Carere-Comes, T. (2007). Bodily holding in the dialogic-dialectical approach. Independent Practice. *Journal of Psychotherapy Integration: 17*(1), 93–110. https://doi.org/10.1037/1053-0479.17.1.93

Colgan, D. D., Christopher, M., Michael, P., & Wahbeh, H. (2016). The body scan and mindful breathing among veterans with PTSD: Type of intervention moderates the realtionship between changes in mindfulness and post-treatment depression. *Mindfulness :* 7(2). https://doi.org/10.1007/s12671-015-0453-0

Cortes-Vazquez. G.. Adriaanse, M., Burchell, G. L., Ostelo, R., Panayiotou, G., & Vlemincx, E. (2024). Virtual reality breathing interventions for mental health: A systematic review and meta-analysis of randomized controlled trials. *Applied Psychophysiology and Biofeedback: 49*: 1–21. https://doi.org/10.1007/s10484-023-09611-4

Duros, P., & Crowley, D. (2014). The body comes to therapy too. *Clinical Social Work Journal, 42*, 237–246. https://doi.org/10.1007/s10615-014-0486-1

Fincham, G. W., Strauss, C., Montero-Marin, J., & Cavanagh, K. (2023). Effect of breathwork on stress and mental health: A meta-analysis of randomised-controlled trials. *Scientific Reports, 13*(1), 432. https://doi.org/10.1038/s41598-022-27247-y

Kabat-Zinn, J. (2002). Commentary on Majumdar et al.: Mindfulness meditation and health. *Journal of Alternative and Complementary, Medicine, 8*(6), 731–735.

Kabri, F., & Surya, J. (2023). The effect of mindful breathing and mindful sitting practices on academic stress of nanyang shi hui high school. Students in Medan. *Journal of Research and Community Service, 4*(10), pe-ISSN: 2797-6068 and p-ISSN: 2777-0915.

Komariah, M., Ibrahim, K., Pahria, T., Rahayuwati, L., & Somantri, I. (2023). Effect of mindfulness breathing meditation on depression, anxiety, and stress: A randomized controlled trial among university students. *Healthcare, 11*(26), 1–13. https://doi.org/10.3390/healthcare11010026

Laborde, S., Mosley, E., & Thayer, J. F. (2017). Heart rate variability and cardiac vagal tone in psychophysiological research—Recommendations for experiment planning, data analysis, and data reporting. *Frontiers in Psychology, 8.* https://www.frontiersin.org/articles/https://doi.org/10.3389/fpsyg.2017.00213

Marotta, J. (2013). *50 Mindful Steps to Self-Esteem.* New Harbinger Publications, Inc.

Mehling, W., Gopisetty, V., Daubenmier, J., Price, C., Hecht, F., & Stewart, A. (2008). Body awareness: Construct and self-report measures. *Plus One, 4*(5), 1–18.

Pichot, T. (2012). *Animal assisted brief therapy: A Solution focused approach.* Routledge.

Pothis, J., Ramu, K., Annamalai, G., Loganathan, R., & Poornachandran, K. (2024). A study protocol for a randomized controlled trial on immediate effect of cooling breathing techniques in generalized anxiety disorder. *World Journal of Biology Pharmacy and Health Sciences, 19*(03), 612–617. https://doi.org/10.30574/wjbphs.2024.19.3.0692

Pozuelos, J. P., Mead, B. R., Rueda, M. R., & Malinowski, P. (2019). Short-term mindful breath awareness training improves inhibitory control and response monitoring. In N. Srinivasan (Ed.), *Progress in brain research* (Vol. 244, pp. 137–163). Elsevier. https://doi.org/10.1016/bs.pbr.2018.10.019

Rothschild, B. (2002) *Body psychotherapy without touch: applications for trauma therapy.* Chapter in Staunton, T. Body psychotherapy. London: Brunner Routledge. p. 101–115

Russo, M. A., Santarelli, D. M., & O'Rourke, D. (2017). The physiological effects of slow breathing in the healthy human. *Breathe, 13*(4), 298–309.

Shaw, R. (2003). *The embodied psychotherapist*. Brunner-Routledge.

Steinmane. V., & Fernate. A. (2025). The effect of breathing exercises on adults' sleep quality: An intervention that works. *Frontiers in Sleep, 4*, 1603713. Open Access: 1–5. https://doi.org/10.3389/frsle.2025.1603713

Tsai, L. T. J., Lai, J. S., Lee, S. H., Chen, Y. M., Lan, C., Yang, B. J., et al. (1995). Breathing-coordinated exercise improves the quality of life in hemodialysis patients. *Journal of the American Society of Nephrology, 6*, 1392–1400. https://doi.org/10.1681/ASN.V651392

Vierra, J., Boonla, O., & Prasertsri, P. (2022). Effects of sleep deprivation and 4-7-8 breathing control on heart rate variability, blood pressure, blood glucose, and endothelial function in healthy young adults. *Physiological Reports, 10*(13), Article e15389.

Wolberg, L. R. (1954). *The technique of psychotherapy*. Grune & Stratton.

Wei, M. (2023). Try box breathing to reduce anxiety & stress. This simple breathing technique calms your mind and body. *Psychology Today.* UK Sussex Publishers, LCC. psychologytoday.com/gb/blog/uran-survival/202303/try-box-breating-to-redue-anxiety-aand-stress

Zaccaro, A., Piarulli, A., Laurino, M., Garbella, E., Menicucci, D., Neri, B., & Gemignani, A. (2018). How breath-control can change your life: A systematic review on psycho-physiological correlates of slow breathing. *Frontiers in Human Neuroscience, 12*, 353. https://doi.org/10.3389/fnhum.2018.00353

Zur, O., & Nordmarken, N. (2004). *To touch or not to touch: Rethinking the prohibition on touch in psychotherapy and counseling Clinical and ethical considerations*. Zur Institute.

Zur, O. (2007). Touch in therapy and the standard of care in psychotherapy and counseling: bringing clarity to illusive relationships. *USABP* Journal: 6(2), 37-44.

10

Visualisations, Progressive Muscle Relaxation, and Affirmations

The use of visualisation is a therapeutic strategy that involves using mental images to help manage a client's distress, thereby reducing their psychological and emotional pain.

Roffe et al. (2005) suggest that such visualisations help people make connections between their mind and body, contributing to empowerment, enabling the individual to manage specific difficulties (Roffe et al., 2005). When a client shares their experience using imagery they usually begin by saying what they see, "yet a therapist can encourage them to tune into other senses such as sound, smell, touch and taste" (Hall & Hall, 2006). Furthermore, emotions may also be induced in visualisations (Roffe et al., 2005), allowing them to be expressed and explored, which is highly relevant to the therapeutic process. Such imagery involving imagination (Achterberg, 1985) is often used to bring calmness and alleviate anxiety and pain (Lang & Patt, 1994).

Carl Jung (1875–1961) stressed the importance of imagination for understanding the unconscious mind and worked with his clients to express their "feelings associated with the images. (Hall & Hall, 2006, p. 12). Jung adopted creative strategies such as drawing, painting and mandala artwork so his clients could engage in 'active imagination'

D. Fleet, *Creative Interventions in Counselling and Psychotherapy*, Palgrave Texts in Counselling and Psychotherapy, https://doi.org/10.1007/978-3-032-16609-8_10

which he argued enabled access to the unconscious while awake. Jung (1961) used a non-directive approach while helping his clients explore the symbols in their creative output and asked questions like, 'What comes to mind when you see that symbol?'

The symbols in visualisations "can have a profoundly transformative impact on our psyche. They can be used to undo past conditioning" (Ferrucci, 1982, p. 118) leading to new ways "of thinking", and feeling by "changing our inner attitudes and outer behaviour" (Ferrucci, 1982, p. 120).

Case Study: Sofia

When working with Sofia, I offered a visualisation strategy, which she was happy to engage with. Her current difficulty at work involved being inundated with tasks, leaving her with little time for holidays or free weekends. Even when not at work, she was contacted via texts and emails asking her to prepare for presentations and projects in her free time. This intrusion into her life outside of work hours was having a negative impact on Sofia. When I helped her to assess the time spent thinking about these extra tasks, she realised that her life was currently out of balance, interfering with her relationship with her partner. I asked her if she wanted to use a strategy that involved imagery, and she was happy to give it a try.

I asked her, "If you could stand back and observe yourself…you and your life at this present moment in time, does an image come to mind that would represent your feelings and thoughts on this?" She responded:

Sofia: (active silence, for a few moments) A wave…coming over me.
Therapist: What does that feel like?
S: Powerful…not in a good way…it's too much.
T: Hard to get out of its way?
S: Mmm
(Active silence, I could see Sofia using the space to be in the moment with this image)
T: (Stayed silent and waited for Sofia to speak)
S: I can be the wave…I am the wave.

Useful questions that helped Sofia explore this image:

Q1: What does that feel like being the wave?
Q2: As the wave, what do you want to say?
Would this be loud or quiet?
Q3: As the wave, what might you want to wash away?
Q4: As the wave, what do you want to change?

As Sofia explored these questions she identified with the powerful image of the wave, it became clear that there was a shift in her presence. She spoke more confidently, and the following discussion involved her planning to take an assertive approach with her boss and clearly define her personal boundaries. I support Ferrucci's (1982) stance on imagery as working with this image in the present was transformative for Sofia, bringing a phenomenological shift (Fleet, 2019; Fleet, 2023, p. 38; Fleet et al., 2021). In that moment, she was no longer the victim of circumstances, with her boss not respecting her boundaries. She felt empowered to plan how she would challenge her boss by clearly setting limits. In the following session, Sofia fed back that her and her boss were in a more supportive relationship.

Guided Visualisations

Another way to use imagery in therapy is to guide the client through a visualisation, often using a prepared script. There are countless recorded guided visualisations online to foster self-help listening to a recording, and can be done independently by the client in their home. Some visualisations help with general issues, such as stress, anxiety, sleep difficulties, and relaxation.

Other "visualisation" scripts focus on more specific issues such as post-traumatic stress disorder (PTSD), addressing the symptoms of flashbacks, nightmares and uncontrollable thoughts, such as 'The forest transcript' (published online by PTSD coach online. National Center for PTSD (.gov) @ department of veteran affairs, USA.

https://www.ptsd.va.gov/apps/ptsdcoachonline/tools/relax-through-visualization/pages/files/visualization-the-forest-transcript.pdf) retrieved 31 August 2025.

This visualisation takes the individual on a relaxing walk through a lush forest, helping them connect with their senses of sight, sound, smell, and touch as they imagine walking through the forest, an experience that aims to promote relaxation and peace.

This method can produce vivid images, and the powerful intensity and realness of the images can facilitate calmness and relaxation for the individual. However, when a guided visualisation is used in therapy with the therapist guiding the client, the vivid images can have a powerful intensity which can help move the client into deep emotional exploration (Farr & Victoria, 1990), facilitated by the therapist's prompts and support. Farr and Victoria (1990) stated how such imagery facilitates understanding outer and inner experience, which is a "purposeful use of the imagination"...helping clients "to explore inner processes" (p. 45).

Lynn and Rhue (1988) suggest that the central aim of guided imagery is to calm an individual's mind while also helping them confront negative emotions, such as anxiety and fear, and to develop their understanding by engaging with the five senses.

When working with adults who have experienced sexual abuse as a child, a safe-space visualisation has often been helpful. Palmer (2001) supports this type of visualisation and suggested how creating a safe space can help clients who have experienced abuse, in that it can promote calm. This type of visualisation involves the client and therapist building an internal "safe place" they can return to in their imagination when they feel anxious and/or triggered. The safe-space context could be anything that the client feels is both safe and relaxing. For example, this could be a safe room, a meadow or any context chosen by the client. Once the safe-space exercise begins, the client is asked to describe the space in detail, referencing senses of sight, touch, smell, hearing, and sometimes taste, enabling a more in-depth experience. Once practised in therapy, the client can imagine returning to that space whenever they feel vulnerable or overwhelmed. When practised several times, the client will experience familiarity as they enter their safe 'room' in their imagination.

Anbar (2023) suggested that a safe space can be a physical space or a place they imagine in their mind, which is calm and where they are safe from harm.

I have worked with clients who have experienced abuse as a child who as an adult can experience dissociation when they become anxious. A safe space has proved to be a valuable coping mechanism. Before establishing the space I usually ask 'where do you feel the safest?' Some answer "in my bedroom". Within the session I ask them to describe the room using their senses of sight, touch, sound, and smell, helping to foster a lucid experience. Others have chosen a place outside such as a meadow or a beach. However, I always emphasis that the space belongs to the client and that no one can enter without the client inviting them.

Recently, a client asked me to guide them through a visualisation to help prepare for a challenging task. Hall and Hall (2006) suggested that when imagery emerges spontaneously, it can help clients be more receptive to the process. My approach was to start with a brief relaxation strategy based on progressive muscle relaxation, where I suggested they relax each muscle in turn. Then, I guided the client to use her imagination and visualise herself leaving work. Slowly, step by step, I guided her to approach the task. I then helped her to visualise taking each step so we would be in sync. Upon completing the task, the client reported feeling calm and ready to proceed with her task that evening.

If therapists begin to offer the strategy of guided visualisations to their clients, they may need to be prepared to incorporate this task into therapy sessions, even if a request to do so emerges spontaneously. Often, a client will assume that you will have the skill to create a visualisation in the current moment. If a therapist is prepared to offer this, it can establish trust in the therapeutic relationship.

Another guided visualisation I deliver is for an online group session. This activity combines breathing, the body and the imagination. The strategy asks clients to scan their body and sense where their anxiety/pain/distress sits. Then, to visualise this distress, move up the body until they breathe this out of their mouth. I then suggest they breathe in a calm, healing energy gently through their nose and visualise this moving to the place in the body where their distress sits. I then repeat this four times.

During the visualisation, I speak softly and slowly throughout. In addition to the clients who report feeling relaxed during and after the session, I have also continued to notice that I, as the guide, also, feel relaxed. Again, as I speak, I also imagine the movement of breath from my lower abdomen moving up my body and breathing this out which helps me in my communication, speaking slowly and calmly.

Routinely, the group usually closes their eyes at the beginning and by the end of the visualisation, look visibly more relaxed.

On completion of the task, I suggest, "Now gently move your fingers, your toes, your hands and your feet, and when you are ready, open your eyes".

For a guided visualisation which involves both client and therapist being vocal, it can help for the therapist to ask some helpful, purposeful questions (depending on what the client is describing), including:

What's going on for you right now?
What does X look like?
What does X feel like?
What does X smell like?
What does X taste like (if appropriate)
What can you hear? (how loud/quiet is X?)

A word of caution when intervening with a question in a client's visualisation: the therapist needs to avoid asking too many questions and keep their tone soft, adopting a gentle pace. Hence, the client stays relaxed.

Progressive Muscle Relaxation

Progressive muscle relaxation (PMR) is a technique that involves tensing then relaxing each muscle of the body in turn. This strategy helps individuals to become mindful and manage the tension, promoting a state of calm which aims to alleviate anxiety and depression. Muhammad Khir et al. (2024) stated how PMR is a viable intervention along with other relaxation strategies such as deep breathing to alleviate stress and anxiety.

In my practice with clients, I often draw on the idea of PMR. Depending on the context and the client, sometimes I will facilitate the tension and then relaxation of different muscles. However, at other times,

I will only focus on the relaxation of each muscle, usually starting from the head.

In communication with the client, we decide which option suits them best, and often they will practice this strategy outside of therapy whenever they are distressed or just before sleep. The feedback I have received from clients who find the strategy helpful includes:

> "It feels good to have a strategy where I can begin to take control of my anxiety"
> "It sends me off to more of a relaxed sleep"
> "When I get anxious, it seems to calm me down. Although, sometimes I have to do this twice"
> "I found it hard to do on my own"—in this instance I suggested I could guide the client through this visualisation in a session when needed.

This strategy also works well when facilitating group therapy. For example, I run a group that focuses on abandonment issues. This group session can bring up painful emotions for the clients and at the end of the session I offer a grounding strategy focusing on relaxing each muscle in turn then scanning the body to identify and process any stress, anxiety, pain, or tension using the following script:

> Sit comfortably and gently close your eyes. Focus your mind on your breathing, in…out…in…out…in…out
> Now move your attention to the top of your head, feel your scalp relax, now feel all the muscles in your face soften and relax, like ice melting. Relax the muscles in your neck and shoulders, just let go, feel your shoulders drop. Relax the muscles in your back. Now relax the muscles in your arms, hands and fingers. Relax the muscles in the chest area, feel the muscles soften as you relax further. Now relax the muscles around the stomach area and the hip area, Relax the muscles in the thighs, knees, calves, feet and toes.
> Now scan your body, tune in to any tension, anxiety or pain. Now place your hands on that part of your body.
> See and feel that tension (or pain) moving up your body, up your throat and breathe this tension out of your mouth.
> Now see and feel yourself breathing in a calm, healing

> energy, gently through your nose, and see and feel it
> moving down your body to that place where the tension
> is and mixing with this hurt.
> Let's repeat that, the tension moving up your body, breathing
> this out of your mouth and then breathing in that calm,
> healing energy moving down to that place.
> (I usually repeat this 3 times).
> Now when you are ready, gently move your fingers and
> toes, your hands and feet…and when you are ready,
> gently open your eyes.

When facilitating this relaxation strategy, it is important to speak slowly and softly, as a gentle approach is most suitable.

Affirmations

Affirmations are positive statements used to challenge negative and unhelpful thoughts, thereby combating the critical and negative inner voice. The words in the affirmation can create a self-fulfilling motivation that has a positive impact on an individual's thinking.

Some examples of affirmations which a client can practice daily are:

- I deserve happiness.
- I have value and I matter.
- My self-worth is not determined by others.
- I stop worrying about what might happen and stay in the moment.
- I will get through this.
- I have the power to act and respect my own needs

Although some clients may need help from the therapist in identifying an affirmation to practice daily, others will prefer to come up with their own affirmation. Whatever works best for the client is usually the best option.

Novia (2025) suggested how affirmations strengthen adaptive thinking, reduce destructive psychological impacts, and increase "life satisfaction by reinforcing autonomy, self-acceptance, personal development and life purpose" (p.24). Furthermore, Novia (2025) goes on to say how affirmations reshape "thought patterns, fostering creativity and strengthening problem-solving skills" (p. 24).

Tiwari et al. (2024) support Novia's suggestion of the positive impact of affirmations and argue that individuals who use positive affirmations regularly can achieve continued self-integrity, bringing high life satisfaction and sustained happiness.

Sherman et al. (2020) suggested that self-affirmations can minimise the consequences of a psychological threat, helping the individual create a more "positive narrative" (Southwick & Charney, 2018), which in turn helps them cope and foster resilience when faced with life difficulties.

A word of caution regarding the use of affirmations: not all clients will be open to using this strategy. Therefore, the therapist needs to present this approach as an offer and respect the client's decision to opt out. I have had some clients where affirmations have helped them, and others say, "Oh, that's not for me...can't picture myself talking in a mirror...just not my cup of tea".

In summary, the strategies of visualisations, progressive muscle relaxation, and affirmations can be offered to clients to help with emotional and psychological distress. From a pluralistic perspective, the decision to use a strategy will be agreed collaboratively between therapist and client. These exercises can be either facilitated by the therapist in sessions or practised by clients at home between sessions. Continual client feedback, achieved by adopting a dialogical approach where the therapist asks purposeful questions, helps monitor the strategy's effectiveness and identify any necessary adjustments to ensure the client gains the optimal benefit.

In conclusion, this text has presented a range of creative methods from a pluralistic approach for therapists to offer clients who are open to working creatively. Creative methods can help clients explore and express their thoughts and emotions through artistic expression. Utilising various art forms, including symbolic images, photographs, objects, drawing, painting, free writing, music, dreams, visualisations, and working with sensory experiences, can help clients express thoughts and emotions that were previously difficult to articulate.

An important consideration is that a client does not have to be artistic to engage with creative methods, as the aim is to help a client express their thoughts and feelings that are often associated with inner distress. Furthermore, the symbolic meaning associated with the client's creative expression can often access 'edge of awareness' and unconscious experience, helping the client to express previously unexpressed issues.

From a personal perspective, I continue to work creatively with clients who are happy to work that way, and have witnessed them express previously unresolved thoughts and feelings, begin to manage their anxiety, ease their depression, gain insight, improve their self-esteem, and develop coping skills.

References

Achterberg, J. (1985). *Imagery in healing: Shamanism in modern medicine.* Shambhala.

Anbar, R. D. (2023). *Growth within and outside of a safe space.* psychologytoday.com/gb/blog/understanding-hypnosis/202307/growth-withiand-outside-of-a-safe-space, retrieved 20 September, 2023.

Farr, C., & Victoria, B. C. (1990). A study of the guided imagery process: Awareness and the discovery of personal meaning. *Canadian Journal of Counselling/Revue Canadienne de Counseling, 24*(1), 45–52.

Ferrucci, P. (1982). *What we may be. Techniques for psychological and spiritual growth.* Library of Congress Cataloging in Publication Data. J. P. Tarcher, Inc. First Edition. CA 90069. USA. ISBN 0-87477-192-7 AACR2.

Fleet, D. (2023). *Pluralistic sand-tray therapy—Humanistic principles for working creatively with adult clients.* Routledge: Taylor & Francis Group.

Fleet, D., Reeves, A., Burton, A., & DasGupta, M. P. (2021). Transformation hidden in the sand: A pluralistic theoretical framework using sand-tray with adult clients. First published online (14 June, 2021). *Journal of Creativity in Mental Health.* https://doi.org/10.1080/15401383.2021.1936738

Fleet, D. (2019). *Transformation hidden in the sand: Developing a theoretical frame-work using a sand-tray interventions with adult clients* (Doctoral thesis). Staffordshire University. Stoke-on-Trent. Available from Ethos STORE—Staffordshire Online Repository. http://eprints.staffs.ac.uk/id/eprnt/5763

Hall, E., & Hall, C. (2006). *Guided imagery. Creative interventions in counselling & psychotherapy.* SAGE Publications Ltd. ISBN-10 1-4129-0148-0
Jung, C. G. (1961). *Memories, dreams and reflections.* (Ed. Aniela Jaffe). Random House.
Novia, A. Z. (2025). Positive affirmation self-talk, impacts on well-being, when and how to start doing it. *International Journal of Social Health, 4*(1), 24–31. https://ijsh.ph/index.php/rp
Palmer, S. E., Brown, R. A., Rae-Grant, N. I., & Loughlin, J. (2001). Survivors of childhood abuse: Their reported experiences with professional help. *Social Work*, 46, 136–145.
Roffe, L., Schmid, T., & Ernst, E. (2005). A systematic review of guided imagery as an adjuvant cancer therapy. *Psycho-Oncology, 14*, 607–617. Published online 13 January 2005 in Wiley InterScience (www.interscience.wiley.com). https://doi.org/10.1002/pon.889
Sherman, D. K., Lokhande, M., Müller, T., & Cohen, G. L. (2020a). Self-affirmation interventions. *Handbook of Wise Interventions: How Social-Psychological Insights Can Help Solve Problems*, 63–99.
Southwick, S. M., & Charney, D. S. (2018). *Resilience: The science of mastering life's greatest challenges.* Cambridge University Press.
Tiwari, G. K., Shukla, A., Macorya, A. K., Singh, A., & Choudhary, A. (2024). The independent and interdependent self-affirmations in action: Understanding their dynamics in India during the early phase of the COVID-19 lockdown. *Journal of Psychological Perspective, 6*(1), 21–38.
Lang, S., & Patt, R. B. (1994). *You don't have to suffer: A complete guide to relieving cancer pain for patients and their families.* Oxford University Press.
Lynn, S. J., & Rhue, J. W. (1988). Fantasy proneness: Hypnosis, developmental antecedents, and psychopathology. *American Psychologist, 43*, 35–44.
Muhammad Khir, S., Wan Mohd Yunus, W. M. A., Mahmud, N., Wang, R., Panatik, S. A., Mohd Sukor, M. S., & Nordin, N. A. (2024). Efficacy of progressive muscle relaxation in adults for stress, anxiety, and depression: A systematic review. *Psychology Research and Behavior Management, 17*, 345–365. https://doi.org/10.2147/PRBM.S437277

Index

D. Fleet, *Creative Interventions in Counselling and Psychotherapy*, Palgrave Texts in Counselling and Psychotherapy, https://doi.org/10.1007/978-3-032-16609-8

www.ingramcontent.com/pod-product-compliance
Ingram Content Group UK Ltd.
Pitfield, Milton Keynes, MK11 3LW, UK
UKHW020044200926
475650UK00005B/73
* 9 7 8 3 0 3 2 1 6 6 0 8 1 *